SIR HALLEY STEWART TRUST: LECTURES

Volume 6

RICH MAN, POOR MAN

RICH MAN, POOR MAN

JOHN HILTON

Routledge
Taylor & Francis Group
LONDON AND NEW YORK

First published in 1944 by George Allen & Unwin Ltd.

This edition first published in 2025
by Routledge
4 Park Square, Milton Park, Abingdon, Oxon OX14 4RN

and by Routledge
605 Third Avenue, New York, NY 10158

Routledge is an imprint of the Taylor & Francis Group, an informa business

© 1944 Sir Halley Stewart Trust

All rights reserved. No part of this book may be reprinted or reproduced or utilised in any form or by any electronic, mechanical, or other means, now known or hereafter invented, including photocopying and recording, or in any information storage or retrieval system, without permission in writing from the publishers.

Trademark notice: Product or corporate names may be trademarks or registered trademarks, and are used only for identification and explanation without intent to infringe.

British Library Cataloguing in Publication Data
A catalogue record for this book is available from the British Library

ISBN: 978-1-032-88942-9 (Set)
ISBN: 978-1-032-88079-2 (Volume 6) (hbk)
ISBN: 978-1-032-88090-7 (Volume 6) (pbk)
ISBN: 978-1-003-53614-7 (Volume 6) (ebk)

DOI: 10.4324/9781003536147

Publisher's Note
The publisher has gone to great lengths to ensure the quality of this reprint but points out that some imperfections in the original copies may be apparent.

Disclaimer
The publisher has made every effort to trace copyright holders and would welcome correspondence from those they have been unable to trace.

This book is a re-issue originally published in 1944. The language used and views portrayed are a reflection of its era and no offence is meant by the Publishers to any reader by this re-publication.

THE
SIR HALLEY STEWART TRUST

★

FOUNDED 15TH DECEMBER 1924
FOR RESEARCH TOWARDS THE CHRISTIAN IDEAL IN ALL
SOCIAL LIFE

TRUSTEES:
BERNARD HALLEY STEWART, M.A., M.D., *President.*
SIR P. MALCOLM STEWART, BART, LL.D., J.P.,
 Treasurer.
SIR PERCY ALDEN, M.A., *Chairman.*
SIDNEY MALCOLM BERRY, M.A., D.D.
THOMAS HYWEL HUGHES, M.A., D.LITT., D.D.
ALBERT PEEL, M.A., D.LITT.
HAROLD BEAUMONT SHEPHEARD, M.A.
STANLEY UNWIN.

The objects of the Trust are *in general:*

To advance religion; to advance education; to relieve poverty; to promote other Charitable purposes beneficial to the community, and *in particular:*

1. To assist in the discovery of the best means by which "the mind of Christ" may be applied to extending the Kingdom of God by the prevention and removal of human misery;
2. To assist in the study of our Lord's life and teaching in their explicit and implicit application to the social relationships of man;
3. To express the mind of Christ in the realization of the Kingdom of God upon earth and in a national and a world-wide brotherhood;

For example:

For every Individual by furthering such favourable opportunities of education, service, and leisure as shall enable him or her most perfectly to develop the body, mind, and spirit:

In all Social Life, whether domestic, industrial, or national, by securing a just environment, and

In International Relationships, by fostering good will between all races, tribes, peoples, and nations so as to secure the fulfilment of the hope of "peace on earth";

4. To provide fees for a Lecture or Lectures annually and prizes for essays or other written compositions, and to pay for their publication and distribution;

5. To provide, maintain, and assist Lectures and Research work in Social, Economic, Psychological, Medical, Surgical, or Educational subjects;

6. To make grants to Libraries;

7. To assist publications exclusively connected with the objects of the Trust (not being newspapers or exclusively denominational);

8. To make grants to and co-operate with Societies, Organizations, and Persons engaged in the furtherance of Charitable objects similar to the objects of the Trust;

9. To use the foregoing and any such other method, whether of a like nature or not, as are lawful and reasonable and appropriate for the furtherance of the objects of the Trust.

The income of the Trust may not be used for dogmatic, theological, or ecclesiastical purposes other than the cult of the Science of God as manifest in man in the Son of Man in the person and teaching of our Lord, "The Word of God," Who "liveth and abideth forever."

SIR HALLEY STEWART LECTURES, 1938

RICH MAN, POOR MAN

by

PROFESSOR

John Hilton

M.A.

With a foreword by
SIR WILLIAM BEVERIDGE, K.C.B.

LONDON
George Allen & Unwin Ltd
MUSEUM STREET

FIRST PUBLISHED IN SEPTEMBER 1944
SECOND IMPRESSION JANUARY 1945

ALL RIGHTS RESERVED

PRINTED IN GREAT BRITAIN
in 12-*Point Old Face Type*
BY UNWIN BROTHERS LIMITED
WOKING

FOREWORD

THE untimely death of John Hilton left the final proofs of this volume uncorrected. I have been asked to write a brief foreword, to say this and other things. I welcome the invitation, for more reasons than one.

First, that I may pay a tribute to the author. John Hilton was one whose life and activity from beginning to end kept him in touch with human realities, with the experiences, aspirations and problems of ordinary men and women. To familiarity with life under many different conditions he added insight, knowledge, humanity and humour.

Second, because the Sir Halley Stewart lectures printed in this volume and delivered in the last year before the present war illuminate one side of our economic structure as it stood then. They throw into relief an inequality of fortune to which we should determine never to return, but to which we may return if we lack determination.

Third, because much of what John Hilton says in his final chapter on "This Thing's to do," leads up directly to the proposals for Social Security which have been my chief concern of recent years.

"It has been put to me so often I feel I must believe it, that what our millions want above all else is security against destitution in the event of a mishap.

"Yet I am not wholly convinced. Greater security, certainly. I have pleaded for it in previous chapters. Accident, sickness, and unemployment are public concerns and ought never

to be tolerated as private visitations. But I beg
leave to doubt whether peace of mind and social
health can ever come from mere security against
destitution. We should strive, also, if we are to
have personal happiness and social health, for a
state of affairs in which the typical family has
sums of its own with which to further its own
fancies and fortune, and from which to learn
something of the technique of firmly holding and
wisely using personal property."

The first part of this quotation, coming from a
man of John Hilton's unrivalled knowledge, is
authoritative. Written in 1938, it is confirmed by
the amazing popular response given three years
later to my Report on Social Insurance and Allied
Services. But the second part of the quotation is
nearly as important, and is equally regarded in that
Report, in that the Report provides for security
without a means-test. Omission of a means-test is an
essential condition of leaving to the individual
incentive and initiative to add for himself to the
minimum provision made by the State. It is a condition of leaving him responsibility and freedom in
planning his own life.

I do not suggest that John Hilton would have
agreed with every detail of what is proposed in my
Plan for Social Security. On the contrary, he raises
directly the question, which has been raised by
other serious students of social conditions, whether
a fixed insurance contribution without reference to
means is necessary and right. He suggests a contribution graded by income as in the New Zealand
Security Scheme. There are strong arguments for
this method of financing Security, though I believe

that the arguments on the other side outweigh them. That is to say, for the reasons set out in my Report, I believe that an insurance contribution as I suggest it without reference to means should be retained as part of the finance of the Security Scheme. But one of the justifications of the relatively high compulsory insurance contribution that I propose, is that it should be comprehensive of every purpose, including funerals, for which people feel bound at all costs to provide, and that there should be no pressure upon persons of limited means to spend money on voluntary insurance beyond their means. That there was such pressure in the period to which the Sir Halley Stewart Lecture relates is proved by the continuing high rates of lapses and excessive funeral provision under industrial assurance.

There is here another point of contact between John Hilton's lectures written in 1938 and the proposals of my Report in 1942. His primary theme, as he points out, is not privation and want, but the unequal distribution of wealth and the question of why so few people have any money in hand, why three out of every four adults in this country at the time when he was writing, possessed less than £100. In answering this question, John Hilton naturally does not ignore the fact that persons of limited means often spend some of their money on unessentials. What has happened to the additional purchasing power which has come to most people in Britain, through technical advance since the first World War as before it? Why has not more of this new wealth been saved?

"Well a good deal of it has gone, of course, in better feeding and clothing and housing and furnishing and reading and holidaying—and quite right too. But it has also gone, along with what was already going in such directions, on pools, perms and pints; on cigarettes, cinemas and singles-and-splashes; on turnstiles, totalizators, and twiddlems: and on all manner of two pennyworths of this and that."

And some of it has gone in buying goods under extravagant or dubious systems of hire-purchases or on burial insurance. John Hilton naturally has much to say on this last item, and makes the exact proposal later included in my Report that funeral benefit should "go on the health card." He urges that high on our list of expedients for increasing the capacity of the people to save, must come the stopping of waste in the existing provisions for saving. At present this particular form of waste by industrial assurance is entrenched in the administration of health insurance.

John Hilton's theme, as I have said, is not simply privation and want, but the unequal distribution of wealth. The former inequalities have been largely reduced during the war, though fresh inequalities have developed as between the fighting forces and others. But these will come to an end presumably with the War. The question of how far we shall then proceed in redistribution of income and towards abolition of extreme inequalities of wealth is one of the central issues for to-morrow. To the understanding of this issue John Hilton's lectures are a vital contribution.

December 24, 1943   W. H. BEVERIDGE

CONTENTS

RICH MAN, POOR MAN

CHAPTER I

A BIT OF MONEY

WE inhabitants of the British Isles own among us an ever-increasing amount of private wealth. If it were equally divided it would come to about £1,500 per typical family. But it is not equally divided. It is in truth owned most unequally. A few among us have, in the vulgar phrase, "tons of money." A fair number have what is spoken of as "a tidy bit." but masses of us own nothing to speak of—or less than nothing.

It is time someone asked afresh how it comes about that this is so. Why are the rich so rich and the poor so poor and the in-betweens so in-between? What are the facts? What are the forces shaping the facts? In particular how does it come about that so many of our people own next to nothing or less than nothing of the aggregate wealth of our land, and can think of no way of ever possessing as much as fifty pounds except by backing the right two horses in a "double" or winning a prize in the pools? That is the task I am here undertaking.

First, a personal word. My interest in these questions goes back a long way. As a very small boy making a great clatter on the flagged pavements of Bolton with my iron-shod clogs I thought of those who had money or who came in for money as people of quite another world from mine.

They lived and moved and had their being, these marvellous creatures, in their own exalted regions. I knew they existed, just as I knew a lot of other things of which I read in books. But it was book knowledge. My sort and their sort had no contacts. They didn't tread any flagstones on which I walked. Our worlds were worlds apart.

So sharp was this sense of separateness that on those occasions when there was pointed out to me someone who was said to have money I think I didn't really believe it. I had towards it the same feeling that I remember to have had towards a woman I heard on the tram telling the man next her that she'd been to Venice.

Venice! I didn't set her down a liar. Not exactly. But I thought she must be putting it on a bit and probably making it up. Real people who'd really been to Venice didn't ride on any tram of mine. Nor did real people who really had great possessions.

As I got on a little, however, I found myself now and then touching elbows with persons who had what's called "private means."

I didn't find that out all at once. The people I was getting on arguing terms with never boasted their possessions. They just took their means as a matter of course; and anyhow no English gentleman ever speaks of his income or its origin. But little by little I came to realize that so-and-so had a private fortune of round about fifty thousand pounds, left him by his grandma; and there was another ten thousand or so to come when his Uncle Charles Henry died. Meanwhile, an odd thousand or two dribbled along when some cousin or aunt passed away.

Now, you do not grasp the reality of people of another order or status until you meet them in the flesh—I do not anyway—and for that reason it was not until now that it began to sink into me that there really were flesh-and-blood knowable people who not only had money but whose life was one of coming in for money and of living on the money they had come in for; or rather living on the income from it and leaving it to others when they died.

Let me say at once that most of those I came to know worked and earned as well as owned and spent. One or two even worked without earning: in what is called "public work." They seemed to me to be mostly giving to the world as much as they took from it—value for value and perhaps a bit more.

There were, of course, others. I knew that. There were others who lounged and roystered and racketed their way through life. But that sort never came my way. I knew of them: but again it was only book knowledge. Or rather it was magazine knowledge. I would read of them in the illustrated pages of the society weeklies when I went to have a tooth out. Perhaps that is why any outbreak of them in the headlines even now gives me a pain in the neck. A sort of mnemonic neuralgia.

The ones I was coming to know gave, as I say, value for value. But even the best and dearest of them dwelt in a monetary world that was as foreign to me as my world was to them.

Mr. Middleton Murry has told how, when he was just beginning to make a name but hadn't begun to make ends meet, he was having tea at the home of a well-to-do lady, patroness of the arts. She said, "You look worried, what's the matter?" He tried to pass it off. She pressed him, saying, "And I can guess what it is you're worried about: it's money." At length he admitted it. She said, "But that's very silly of you. Why worry? Do as I always do. Sell some of your securities."

That is more than a story: it is a parable. It is the parable of how one-twentieth of the world doesn't know how the other nineteen-twentieths live. She had no idea, poor ignorant lass, that the vast majority of people have never as much as seen a security, much less owned one.

The multitude know nothing of securities. Some have a little in the Post Office, in Savings Certificates, in a Trustee Savings Bank, or in the Co-op.; some own (more or less) the house they live in; many own household goods and gear; some have an endowment policy; and some have small businesses whose stock-in-trade and goodwill is worth a little. Property of these kinds you'll find here and there among the multitude. But securities—or anything whatsoever that you'll find on the finance page of your daily paper—no.

I would like to know what proportion of the readers of the popular daily papers ever look at the finance page. Is it one in twenty? Or one in fifty? Is it more than one in a hundred?

"Here and there" among the multitude, I have just said, you will find possessions. But only "here and there." The rest have no savings at all, no fall-back whatsoever in times of dire need, nothing at all in hand with which to pay cash for any substantial article or to take advantage of a bargain or seize an opening; and not a friend or kinsman able and willing to lend. Nothing in the family; and nothing in the clan.

I am going to ask how they come to be like that; and whose fault it is; and whether it is worse or better than it was; and what it means; and what is to be done about it—if anything.

But, first, what are the facts? How many of us have substantial fortunes? How many of us have more modest fortunes of various sizes? How many of us live from hand to mouth? How many of us live in debt?

Alas! we know for certain very little. On these vital matters we are badly ignorant. We know a fair amount about the better-off; but we know next to nothing about the poorer-off.

We know a good deal about the earnings and spendings of Tom and Dick and Harry; but next to nothing about their ownings and owings. Those who make house-to-house Budget enquiries, whether official or unofficial, ask all sorts of questions about

how the family income is spent; but they never, or
very rarely, ask anything about savings or debts.
They know it would not be liked, and would not
elicit the truth. So the most one can do is to make
guesses based on such glimpses as one can get
from public or private sources.

What we do know a good deal about is the circumstances of those who have anything from £100
upwards to their name. And we know about that
section of our populace for two reasons.

The first is that when we die the tax-gatherer
wants to know whether we have left, all told and
on balance, as much as £100. If we have, then he
wants—and he gets—full particulars.

He has to be told everything about everything.
About our household goods—pictures, china, ap-
parel, books, plate, jewels, etc.; about our cash in
hand or at the bank; about any stocks or shares or
savings certificates; about any money in our name
at the Post Office or in the Club or the Co-op;
about all money owing to us; about any land or
property we may more or less own; about stock-in-
trade, implements, live-stock and so on; about
goodwills; about our insurance policies; about any
gifts we have been making; about our debts . . .
in fact about anything and everything that might
make an item in the full tale of our personal possessions.

Very little can escape the Probate Officer. Very
little does. And when his assessments and taxation
levies are completed he makes returns to his head-

quarters and these returns are worked up into the annual probate statistics.

That is how we come to have the material from which to know so much about the wealth-ownership of those who are worth, all told and on balance, anything from £100 upwards.

"But come," you may say, "that cannot be right! You cannot take the figures of what people leave at death as telling what people are worth in life! Those who die are mostly getting on in years. If you use the property-at-death figures for property-in-life you will be hopelessly wide of the mark!"

Of course you will. If you took just the probate statistics and used them raw you would get the pattern all askew. You must not do that. What you must start from is that, although it is mostly the old who die, yet all the time a certain number of persons of all ages and all conditions are also dying; and every person who dies and whose estate is looked into by the revenue officer affords a glimpse into the wealth-ownership position of all persons of that age. Once grasp that, and start a set of special calculations based upon it, and you can deduce the fortunes of the living from the leavings of those who die.

There are, let me say, certain snags and catches. For instance, it may well be that those who die before their time are of rather poorer stock and therefore poorer earnings and accumulating capacity than the average. They may be somewhat impoverished by prior sickness. To that extent what they own may be not quite typical or representative of what is owned by the living of their age. But you can, if you like, make what allowance you think fit for that. I do not think you will need to allow nearly as much as you might suppose.

It is quite certain, too, that the lowly and the badly-off tend to die younger than the lofty and the well-to-do. So you must not judge the financial position of all who are aged, say, thirty by those who die aged thirty or you will be below the mark. You must allow for the different death-rates of richer and poorer. You must also keep an eye on the differences in mortality rates of men and women.

If you watch these points you can allow for them. The information is all to hand. Thereupon you can do sums which will give you, from the raw probate figures of the dead, a picture of wealth distribution among the living that is free of most of the distortions due to death not falling quite impartially, age by age, on rich and poor, on labourer and lawyer, and on man and woman.

This operation of deducing wealth distribution among the living from what is left by those who die has been worked at by a long line of statisticians. Each has further refined the process. Latest in the long line have been Professor Daniels and Mr. H. Campion of Manchester University. Their joint work, *The Distribution of the National Capital*, was published by the Manchester University Press in 1936.

Since Professor Daniels's lamented death, Mr. Campion, who is the Reader in Economic Statistics in the University of Manchester, has further de-

veloped the technique of the matter and has brought
the analysis up to the latest date for which official
returns are available.

His account of these later researches was recently
published by the Oxford University Press in a book
entitled *Public and Private Property in Great Britain*.
I am indebted to Mr. Campion for these later
results and for advice on various aspects of my own
theme—advice which may not have always borne
fruit in my words.

So for such facts as I may need concerning
wealth distribution among persons worth £100 and
more I merely dip into Daniels and Campion, or
into Campion, and lift what I want. If you wish to
know more of the way in which the figures are
arrived at, you must consult one or both of the books
I have mentioned.

The master figure we need at the outset is the
proportion of those among our adult populace (or
say rather those over 25) who if they sold up all
they have in the world, cashed in all their savings
and insurances, paid their debts, and counted up the
net balance of their worldly wealth, would turn out
to be worth £100 or more.

The proportion is startling. It is in the region of
only 25 per cent. Only about one-quarter of our
adult people possess, on balance, as much as £100.
The remaining three-quarters have less than £100
worth of this world's goods to their name.

That is persons: individuals. But to most people
private wealth in terms of individuals does not

mean very much. When one thinks of property one's thoughts willy-nilly run to family property. Then can we convert Campion's individual figure to a family figure?

It is not an easy operation. Families are of so many widely different sorts and sizes that talk of wealth per family or per household cannot have any sort of precision. There are, among others, widows and widowers, bachelors and spinsters, to be reckoned with. But let us try to fix our mind on what we might call a typical or representative sort of family: one with a husband and wife at the head. Then the problem is to judge from what we know about the separate possessions of men and women the truth about the joint possessions of husbands and wives.

We know that while the fraction of all persons worth £100 and more is about one-quarter of the adult population, the proportion for men is about 30 per cent and for women about 20 per cent. We know, therefore, that although the average woman has less to her name than the average man, she is by no means propertyless. But who knows the proportion of homes in which parental savings are in the husband's name only or in the wife's name only, and the proportion in which they are split between the two? As with most questions in this field of social enquiry, no one knows.

So if we want to express wealth distribution in terms of families we must do some guessing. I am going to venture a guess or two. If you will let me assume, as I think I may, that in the great majority of not-too-well-off households the family possessions are in the name of one or other of the parents (rather than split between them), and if you are prepared to use "family" in a free and easy sense without being too pernickety about definition (call it "household" if you like), then I think a likely enough guess can be made.

My guess is that of the twelve million or so "families" in our land four million could show—if they sold up, cashed in, realized at a fair price on their insurances, paid their debts, and put their whole fortunes on the table—£100 or over of parental wealth. Eight million families, if my guess be right, would not be able to show as much as £100.

You may yourself, after reflection upon the data, think the figure of eight million too high or too low. I myself think it probably as near as makes no matter.

Of the ownings of families above the £100 mark, we can know a good deal; but how much can we know about that eight million families who are below the £100 mark? Must we give up any hope of even guessing about them? Not altogether, I think. Straightway I will make a guess for which I will give grounds later. It is that of the eight million families who are worth less than £100, it is probable that four million are worth somewhere between an odd pound or two and a round hundred, and four million are either just square with nothing in hand or are in debt for a larger or smaller amount.

I hope I have not been unduly tempted towards these proportions because of the neatness of the pattern they give. It seems too straightforward to be true that family ownings should fall into three such simply stated and easily remembered equal categories: four million families with £100 and over, four million with anything from a pound or two up to nearly £100, and four million with no more than they stand up in or sit down at—if that. Perhaps the lure of such a simplicity has led me just a little from the strait and narrow path of unbiased estimating. But not far, I hope.

My concern, as I say, is to be mostly with the eight million families whose parental wealth is less than £100. None the less, I think we must take a glance, more than a glance indeed, at the four million who are at or above the £100 mark, and rather especially at the very wealthy ones among them; for clearly the opulence at the top may have some bearing, must have some bearing, on the indigence down below. It may even have some bearing on the improvidence down below.

But here I must abandon any attempt to talk in terms of "families." I may flatter myself that I know something of how the nest-egg is cared for in working-class households, but I know next to nothing of how the family fortunes are held among the well-to-do. So I must accept Mr. Campion's individual figures and forbear any tying of them into family bundles.

Let us start at the pinnacle. I say the pinnacle

because it is convenient to think of this part of the wealth-distribution problem in the image of a pyramid. At the base are the millions of those with nothing or less than nothing, and in ever-narrowing higher strata are the fewer and fewer numbers who have greater and greater possessions—up to the shining pinnacle, the platinum point, where the really opulent abide. You can, of course, think of families, too, in that pyramid form if you like; but the measurements are available for persons only.

Starting at the top, then, let us look at those who are worth more than £100,000. They number twelve or thirteen thousand persons. They are a tiny fraction of our adult population—one in two thousand—but they own among them nearly one-fifth (18·0 to 18·8 per cent) of all the property in private hands.

Or take a less exclusive company. Take all those who are worth more than £10,000. They are one-hundredth of our adult population, but they own among them a good deal more than half (54·8 to 56·7 per cent) of all the property in private hands.

You can, of course, if you will consult Campion, know about the middle ranges of the pyramid. I am not re-expounding his analysis. I am only quoting enough to show that the mass of the privately ownable wealth of this country is in very few hands.

We need not as yet be shocked or upset by these facts. I am not sure we need even be startled by them. But we ought to know them, and ask ourselves questions about them. We ought to wonder how it comes about that so many own so little and so few own so much, and what it signifies and portends.

In particular we ought to wonder how it is that eight million of the twelve million families in this ever-wealthier land own among them less than one-twentieth of the personally-ownable wealth of our country. We ought to ask ourselves why four million of them own nothing, and may be more or less chronically in more or less crippling debt.

For the moment, let the larger issues simmer on the hob: for I must redeem my promise to disclose the source of the glimpses and side-lights which led me to my guess of four million for the number of wholly propertyless and in some part debt-ridden families in Great Britian.

There is first the glimpse obtained by the Unemployment Assistance Board. Its investigators pay a monthly visit to every person in receipt of Unemployment Assistance, a visit having for its object, among other things, to ascertain needs and means. Their very mission requires them to ask about savings; and they are likely to be told a good deal about debts. Their knowledge of debt they keep to themselves. Their knowledge of savings is on record.

At a time when there were some 570,000 applicants for Unemployment Assistance:

". . . there were about 10,750[1] applicants (or their wives or husbands) who possessed

---

[1] The printed figure (of 12,500) contains an error. The figure of 10,750 has been furnished to me as a correction by the U.A.B.

capital resources other than that represented by the house which the applicant owned and occupied. The value of this capital is estimated to be about £1,250,000." (Cmd. 5752, page 80.)

So only 10,750 out of 570,000 on the U.A.B. had a little money laid by. They had, on average, this 10,750, about £120 per family. That figure strikes one as astonishingly high. If that is the average, and if the bulk had very little, then a few must have had hundreds of pounds. What a pity we cannot abolish the average from all social statements! What we want to know is not the average, but the dispersion of the ownings among these 10,750 people.

Be that as it may, only one in 53 of these on the books of the U.A.B. had any money in hand. One in 22 also owned, wholly or in part, the house he lived in. What that owning was worth no one knows. A very few not only owned more or less their home but also had a bit of money. All told, one in fifteen had some money in hand or some ownership in the home.

So you may take fourteen-fifteenths of those who fell within the province of the U.A.B. as without any property worth mentioning but their household goods and chattels. I say "within the province of the U.A.B." because I do not want you to think just of the 570,000 who round about that time happened to be on the books of the U.A.B. on a given day but preferably of the 1,250,000 who were

on its books at some time or other during the year;
for any household which had its chief earner on
Unemployment Assistance at one time or another
during a year was likely, I think, to be a household
with resources not much exceeding the resources
of those who happened to be on its books on any
one day.

Think therefore not of 570,000 but of a million
and a quarter; and think of fourteen-fifteenths of
those persons as without any "capital resources"
whatsoever and in some part, of course, burdened
and shackled by debt.

Look next at those who, not being capable of
and available for gainful work, were in receipt of
Public Assistance. They with their dependants
numbered at that time about $1\frac{3}{4}$ million souls,
which means perhaps 400,000 households. They
may interweave and overlap a little with the U.A.B.
personnel, but not, I think, to any great extent.
They can be taken as certainly propertyless and as
probably afflicted in some part by debt.

There you have two of the glimpses of which I
spoke into the numbers of our propertyless households. Already the total looms large. It looms large
even before I mention those on unemployment
benefit proper. I do no more than mention them
because we have no knowledge whatever of their
debt and savings position.

If you should be disposed to say, "Oh, they're
all right. They've mostly got a little in hand," I
ask you in reply why then have we had to be so

careful about any proposal for extending the "waiting period" before benefit begins to be drawn. Suggestions to extend the days of waiting from three to six quickly brought evidence of the suffering it would cause among the innumerable families who had not six days' pay in hand. Is that all nonsense? If not, the bulk of those on benefit have nothing to play with.

And of course I have so far said nothing of those who are earning, but whose earnings have been too small for saving or whose incomes, though ample, have been used or squandered as fast as they were earned. I have said nothing of young people starting out in life with little if anything in hand. I have said nothing of old age pensioners who may be past work. If you add any picture you like to make of the wealthless wage-earners and pensioners to the wealthless unemployed and unemployable you will not hesitate, I think, to accept my guess of four million for families who have no part whatever in the ownership of the aggregate wealth of the nation, and many of whom have less than nothing in that they are fitfully or chronically in debt. You may think it much too low.

The practice of running into debt and the condition of being in debt is not confined to the wage-earners. The small manufacturers, the shopkeepers, and the farmers could contribute their quota to the company of the debt-ridden. Nor is getting into debt and living in debt confined to the poor.

Quite a number of those who live in style live in

debt: some through ill-luck; some because they are
that sort. We cannot help ill-luck and we cannot
altogether help people being that sort. I am not here
asking why we do not have a world without vicissi-
tudes or a race without vices. I am asking rather how
it comes about that two-thirds at least of the families
that comprise our nation are either on the edge of
complete wealthlessness or are, as a mass or as a
class, fitfully or chronically on the debit side of
life's reckonings; in debt to shopkeepers, landlords,
rating authorities, pawnbrokers, tallymen, or money-
lenders; or in debt to kith and kin.

There are many such who are chronically in debt.
But there are others who are in debt at some phase
or other of their lives. Indeed, there is a debit and
credit cycle of life. During some periods we are,
most of us, in the debit phase; in other periods we
are in the credit phase. So you must not think that
people who happen to be in debt or in credit at any
particular time are so set for life. What I am trying
to give is a snapshot of people as they happen to be
at a given moment. I shall say more about that
debit and credit cycle by and by.

So two-thirds of our families own next to nothing
or nothing at all or less than nothing of the privately
ownable wealth of our land. That aggregate of
"privately ownable wealth" is going to be in the
background of much that is to follow, and we ought
to have a notion of its aggregate value. I shall take
as the best for my purpose Mr. Campion's figure of
round about £20,000 million for the total of property

in private hands in the year 1936. The figure excludes, naturally, public property owned by "the authorities" and official bodies.

Twenty thousand million pounds! Such a figure means nothing unless you try to visualize the things and processes whose aggregate value comprise it. Then look out of the window as you go along in the train. Use your eyes and your imagination. Fields, factories, and workshops, and railroads of course; and not only the market value of what you can see of them, but the capital value of what is going on in them. Vehicles of all kinds, ships and trains and cars of all sorts, with their cargoes and the capital value of their earning power. Houses by the million, shops and stores and buildings of all kinds by the hundred thousand, and all that in them is. Coin in hand, in till, and in bank. Scrip representing titles to wealth invested abroad. The catalogue of types of wealth could stretch for pages more; but it will serve for us to see it in the mass as mostly material, tangible, or visible; or, as the capital value of an activity going forward.

Twenty thousand million pounds. Yet one-third of our families have no part nor lot in the ownership of it; and another third has a trumpery amount, not exceeding a hundred pounds per family. The bulk of it is in the hands of a compact cluster of rich people.

Gross privately owned wealth, twenty thousand million: total number of families twelve million. That makes, on average, fifteen hundred pounds per family. A curious thought, that if our land were by some magical conversion to have become suddenly Christianized; if in obedience to Christ's injunction "sell all thou hast and give to the poor," all owning more than the average of worldly possessions could not rest until they had bestowed their surplus on someone with less than the average; and if that were to continue until all were living in about the same accommodation among about the same value of household goods and holding scrip to about the same share of vested property— it is a curious thought that in the event of such a conversion each family in the land would be worth about £1,500. A still more curious thought is that each family would be receiving about a pound a week interest over and above whatever its earnings might be—provided, of course, the dispersal of the wealth's ownership did not lead to the dissolution of its substance!

I have spoken of the wealth pyramid and said it was a useful image of our society as it is. But of course one can conceive of societies with wealth-patterns of other shapes. If, for example, the miracle I have just mentioned were to take place, there would no longer be a pyramid. Our wealth structure would be pictorially more like a flat cake.

Or you could conceive a social order whose pattern was less a pyramid than a football, an order in which the great bulk of families owned round about average fortunes and in which the numbers of those who had less than that fortune fell away rapidly until there were hardly any at zero, and in which no one had more than double the average, and the numbers with double were also very small.

Or you could conceive an economic order to the pattern of a bishop's mitre, in which the numbers of families in each ascending wealth-group were of about equal magnitude, with a little peak of not-very-superior magnates at the crown.

I mention these conceivable varieties so that you shall not think of the pyramid shape as inevitable and eternal. It is in human nature, I know: but human nature is changeable. At any rate, the manifestations of human nature are changeable, particularly in these days of high-pressure propaganda. Within the limits imposed on us by our own make-up our society can be and will be what we want it to be.

If instead of our present inverted peg-top with its platinum tip we prefer the round of the ball or the oval of the egg, we can work towards it. We may never achieve it, but we can get nearer to it than we are to-day.

Throughout recorded history there have been collective efforts to alter the pointed pyramid shape to some other. They are not always fruitful of results. In recent decades, for instance, we have been crowding taxation on the well-to-do; relieving them of large portions of their incomes while they live and large portions of their possessions when they die; and we have been devoting the proceeds in part to social works and services. Has not that process of taking from the rich and giving to the poor altered the shape of the pyramid?

Apparently not, to any marked degree. Certainly the percentage of adults worth £100 and upward nearly doubled between 1914 and 1938. Money is worth less, it is true, but that does not wipe out the improvements in the proportion of those who have a little or a good deal in hand. Looked at from below rather than above, the gain is not quite so impressive. Instead of seven-eighths having less than £100 all told, the proportion has become six-eighths. There has been a change, but not one to make a song about.

Those worth £10,000 and over are more numerous, relatively, than they were in 1914. (In 1938 1·5 per cent of our adult populace instead of just over 0·5 per cent.) But they still in their larger numbers own the same proportion as they did then, just over half, of the personally ownable wealth (about 56 per cent). The very wealthiest, those with over £100,000, are also proportionately more numerous (they have increased from 0·03 per cent to 0·05 per cent), and although the share of the wealth they own has fallen, it has not fallen much. (From about 22·2 to about 18·4 per cent.)

The most marked change has been that the salaried lower-middle classes have considerably increased their relative numbers and relative share of our privately ownable capital. I will put that pictorially by saying that the inverted peg-top has bulged a little at the waist.

Otherwise the shape of the wealth-pyramid has

changed very little. What is significant is not the change but the smallness of it, despite all the taxation of large incomes in life and large fortunes at death. The standard of life for rich and for poor has improved. We have all moved up a peg. But at our somewhat higher elevation we are still a pyramid with a poverty-stricken base and a platinum point.

There are, however, two quite distinct aspects of people's share of worldly goods. I have so far dealt entirely with possessions. But a man or a family can rub along pretty well without great possessions provided there is a fat income coming in. The spendthrift professional man—if such there be!— may live up to his income of £10,000 a year without owning as much as would lie on a sixpence. Edgar Wallace had been making in his latter years £50,000 a year; but when he died was found to be in debt to the tune of £140,000. (Within two years, let me say, the proceeds from his books and plays were enough to clear his debts.) The skilled workman with a safe job at £3 10s. a week with pension attached, or the government clerk on the same or higher pay, may go through life with never so much as £100 in hand and never feel the lack. There is then an income pyramid to be considered as something distinct from the possessions pyramid.

At the point of the income pyramid are ten thousand persons with incomes of over £10,000 a year. Their average income is £22,000 a year per head. They are half of 1 per cent of all income recipients, but they receive 6 per cent of the aggregate income.

At the base of the pyramid are eleven and a half million persons with incomes of less than £2 10s. a week. Their average is £2. They are two-thirds of all the income-receiving population; they receive one-third of the aggregate income. (That takes in the youngsters with their small pay, but on the other hand it leaves out the pensioners with their smaller pay and the unemployed on benefit or dole.)

Now the income pyramid is not nearly so steep as the wealth pyramid. True there are eleven and a half million persons in that bottom group; but there are five million persons within the range of £2 10s. to £5 per week, whose average is £4 per week. There are far more in the "middle classes" of wealth ownership. The income pyramid is more squat than the possessions pyramid, and bulges even more at the waist.

There are two other important things to say about the income pyramid. One is that the analysis I have just given relates to incomes before taxation. The shape of the income pyramid is modified somewhat by the effect of taxation, though not nearly so much as one who thought only of income-tax and surtax might suppose. Do not forget that though direct taxation is heavy on the rich, indirect taxation is heavy on the poor.

How far has the income pyramid changed its shape since, shall we say, before 1914? The conclusion reached by those who have specially examined this matter is that, even allowing for taxation, there has been little change in the distribution pattern. Again we have all moved up a peg. There are more in the technical and administrative middle class. The pyramid has bulged at the waist. But the fatness of the fat incomes and the leanness of the lean incomes are relatively about as they were.

I shall not concern myself much with the income pyramid, except to ask how far low wages are responsible for the wealthlessness of so many millions of families. My concern is to be more with the possessions pyramid. But I must take account of the income pyramid here because since 1914 we have been building up a system of social services in which every insured worker has in the form of insurance rights the equivalent, if you care so to look at it, of personal ownership of a fairly big sum.

A person insured under the Health and Unemployment Insurance Acts is entitled to a life pension of 10s. per week at age 65. It may be twice that amount, for man and wife. Now to buy a life annuity equal to 10s. a week for life from 65 onwards would cost between £250 and £350. With every decade that passes it will cost more, for there are going to be increasingly more old folks living longer.

If you add unemployment benefit and sickness benefit and one or two others, you will find that most adults in this country, though they may own less than £100 in personal savings, own on top of that a right, which would cost them several hundreds of pounds if they tried to buy it with cash, to draw on public funds in case of need or when they reach a certain age.

Of course, they have in part paid for it, by stamps in books and to a smaller extent through direct or indirect taxation. Then are not these contributions in a sense as much accumulations of private wealth as anything put away in the Post Office or the Co-op or the Savings Bank?

Yes, these rights are in a sense personal private property. They give a claim on the community to income of a sort in case of specified calamity or of advancing years. They have made a vast difference to our social and economic texture.

Compared with what they were at the turn of the century our social services are a miracle of collective care and collective kindliness. Compared with what they might well be they are in some respects paltry and mean. If the world can remain at peace we shall, I fancy, feel impelled to make much more generous provision than any we have yet contemplated for those who fall into distress because their wages-income has failed. But it isn't my present purpose to argue that. My concern is with the bearing of the social services upon the distribution of wealth ownership.

It is true that the right to 10s. a week at 65 may be worth as much as £350 in the bank. It is true that the right to a regular weekly payment in case of sickness for a considerable period with free doctoring and medicine and so on may represent, according to age and circumstance, what another

hundred or more pounds in savings could not buy.
It is true that Benefit followed by Assistance in the
event of unemployment may in some cases be
worth what £500 could not buy. It is true that the
right to free elementary education for as many
children as one cares to produce, with perhaps such
oddments in addition as free milk and free dental
examination, may represent what yet another £100
to £500 could not buy. All these things are true in
particular cases, and they must be taken as pro-
foundly modifying the effective pattern of the
possessions pyramid. But it is also true that not
one of our social services represents the *actuality*
of private means, in the sense that a lump sum of
money is available to the insured person, or is at
some point in time paid out to the beneficiary.

Our social services cover a good deal—but not
that. They are one and all weekly driblets to the
necessitous given out on the avowed or tacit assumption that he or she has little or nothing in hand—
and can hardly be expected to have anything in
hand, to meet any emergency.

Are we to say, then, that the continued wealthlessness of so many of our families is a perfectly natural
thing in that we long ago gave up any policy we
may once have had of encouraging the wide dispersal of privately ownable wealth among the populace
and adopted instead the policy of social services in
lieu of private means? Have we been anticipating
Soviet Russia in intentionally creating and per-
petuating a propertyless proletariat—with the differ-

ence that in the one case the nation's property is held and administered by an official class and in the other by a monied class?

I do not think that was the conscious intention. It could hardly have been so over the longish period in which we were trying to make Benefits more and more irrespective of means—trying to make them something supplementary to means. It could hardly have been so when we were busy instituting insurance pensions to be drawn without question as to means or income.

Of course there was even then—in the pre-Means-Test era—less need for the wage-earner to have a due share of the nation's wealth to his private and personal name. But fear of starvation is only one element in the urge to have worldly wealth in personal store. Up to that point certainly the encouragement of hand-to-mouth living for the millions was there neither as intention nor result.

Not until the Means Test for persons long unemployed was there cause to wonder whether something was not going on in the governing mind adverse to the possessing by Tom and Dick and Harry of a share in the nation's wealth. It seemed difficult to believe that the policy of making a careful man part with nearly all his substance before he might have assistance, and of giving assistance at once to one who had spent his money as it came, was uninfluenced by any thought that it was just as well to discourage the holding of riches by the multitude?

It seems inconceivable that in introducing the

Means Test we had not set ourselves to smash saving and owning by the common folk: yet I myself doubt—such queer creatures are we—if that thought entered much into the muddle in our heads at the time. The fact that we painstakingly decided to say nothing about the first £25 of a man's nest-egg and to let him off with a caution and the merest fine for having somewhat larger amounts, and that we agreed to wink at his owning the house he lived in, shows a feeling of being on the edge of something we wanted to avoid.

Whether the effect, as distinct from the intention, was to encourage the notion that to be without means is the right and proper thing for common folk is a question I shall have to look at later. But as for the intention, it is curious to reflect that even as with one hand we were knifing thrift in the back, with the other we were patting it on the shoulder, giving encouragement in the sense of blessing and protecting and fostering the facilities for working-class saving.

The social services have most certainly moderated the income pyramid; but they almost seem to be intensifying the wealth-ownership pyramid. Or is it that other forces, natural or unnatural, are at work keeping the multitude propertyless and forcing or drawing the privately ownable wealth into few hands?

Whichever it be, the fact remains that eight million of our twelve million families have not as much as a hundred pounds to their name and that four of that eight million have on balance neither part nor lot in the massed wealth of this rich country.

But how can that be? Have we not constantly read in our newspapers of that £3,000,000,000 which stood in 1938 to the credit of the "little man," the "small saver," in such institutions as the Post Office, the Trustee Savings Banks, the Building Societies, the Insurance Companies, and so on? The "Little Man's Nest-Egg" one newspaper called it. Another said, "There are ten million working-class families in the country; so, averaged throughout the nation, each family has £300 saved up."

Three hundred pounds per family, and I've been saying that four million families have nothing and another four million have less than £100! Three hundred pounds per family! Is that true? If it is true, then I've been talking mere foolishness. Then what is the matter with it? That is for my next chapter.

CHAPTER II

PUTTING BY

Now and again I run my eye down the "Wills and Bequests" column of my Sunday paper. Here is one for a random week. A gentleman of Cornwall leaves £180,000. In the same week the widow of a clergyman leaves £110,000. A Scottish stockbroker leaves £88,000. A barrister leaves £86,000. And so on down the list to a butcher and a hosiery maker who leave a mere £26,000 each.

Modest fortunes, I know. It just so happened that week. Not a single millionaire. Not even a quarter millionaire. After all, what is £180,000? There must be ten thousand people in our midst who are worth so much and more. Yet I suppose it brought him in about £150 a week. Perhaps more, perhaps less. Without touching the principal, of course. And over and above anything he earned.

Yes, I suppose about £150 a week; for there comes to me one of the first things I remember to have been told about private fortunes. I recall the very time and place: it was in the little play-yard of Mawdsley Street School, Bolton, and I should be about eleven. What I was told by an older and more knowing boy there in the school yard was that every thousand pounds you saved would bring you in a pound a week for ever and ever and ever.

That must have been in the golden days of the

5 per cents. It was certainly before the days of high taxation of incomes and of leavings. But even fifteen shillings a week! For more or less ever and ever! Just because you had saved a thousand pounds! Amazing!

But saved a thousand pounds! I began to wonder how people managed to save a thousand pounds. To us, in my young days, saving meant stinting oneself, going without, being very careful, watching every penny, putting coin to coin, and never drawing unless you could not possibly help it. That was called thrift.

I knew about thrift. My own mother practised it. I used to charge her with the habit of adding it to St. Paul's great trilogy. She used it to make a fourth. Her full, private version was "And now abideth faith, hope, charity, thrift, these four; but the greatest of these is thrift."

So when I was told in the Sunday School and at the Band of Hope that all the great fortunes had been built up by thrift, I knew no grounds for doubting it. Yet quite early, it seems to me now, questionings crept into my mind. I remember a speaker—at the Annual Sermons I think it was—explaining that you became a person of means and eventually a millionaire by going without things; for instance, he said, going without jam if you'd already got butter.

It was there and then that I experienced doubt. For I began trying to reckon how much jam you would have to go without to save a million pounds.

I didn't believe there was so much jam to be gone without in all the world

Of course you *can* save money by walking instead of taking the tram? You *can* save by wearing one collar for a week. If you take care of the pence a certain number of pounds will look after themselves? All that is true. And along that line you can very properly argue that the millionaire saved his million by economizing in larger ways. He didn't buy and run a world-cruising steam yacht; and when people asked him why he did not set up racing stables he told them he had more sense and went on with his money-making and saving.

But that isn't saving a fortune, that is avoiding losing it. You must have a fortune before you can do much in the way of not losing it.

Then how does one come to have a fortune? There was, of course, that city clerk. He had never in his life had more than four pound ten a week, but now, at age sixty-five he was retiring, and it had got about that he was able to retire because he had £5,000 put by. His fellow clerks gave him a little dinner. In thanking them he said: "You have all heard how it is I am able to retire. I dare say you wonder how I have managed it, for you all know what my salary has been. I owe it in great part to my own abstemious and thrifty habits. Even more I owe it to the carefulness and good management of my dear wife. But still more I owe it to the fact that a month ago an aunt of mine died and left me four thousand nine hundred and fifty-seven pounds."

A good story, if an old one; and like all good stories it has a lot of truth in it. But as one may very rightly remark, it hasn't the whole truth. There *have* been people of small income who have saved quite a lot; and anyway, even if the city clerk did inherit nearly all his five thousand from an aunt, someone must have saved it some time or the aunt wouldn't have had it to leave.

Yes, of course. I myself knew a working man, a low-wage working man too, who managed before he retired to save more than four thousand five hundred pounds. He and his wife, I should say. She did sewing and dress-making to help out, but nothing fancy, and in quite a small way. They achieved it by denying themselves and their one child everything but the bare essentials of money-earning and money-saving life. A life many of us would think not worth living: though I dare say it has a queer sort of fun of its own. A life without flourishes or graces or amusements or distractions or holidays—except the amusement of skimping and hoarding. Of course it can be done.

Everyone has come across such cases, or has read of them. I have just turned over some of my press cuttings. Here is one headline: "In Workhouse, but worth £2,000." Here is another: "£1,300 Found in Room of Dead Road-Sweeper." And here is a snippet concerning my native town: "Although dressed in rags when he died in a Bolton lodging-house, Thomas Hamer turned out to be worth £3,000." In a recent L.C.C. Report there is quoted the case of a man in Westminster Poor-House who was found to have in his box savings to the total of £2,400.

We are always reading of such cases; and unless we take care we fall into the error of supposing that therefore they are common. But they are not common. That is why we hear of them: because they are unusual: because they are exceptions to the rule. If they weren't exceptions they wouldn't be in the news, and we shouldn't either read of them or note them for ourselves and then remember them. But because they are exceptions we do remember them, and, that being so, we are apt to quote them and to argue from them. When anyone says in refutation of your general truth, "I'll give you an illustration to the contrary," you can be pretty sure he is going to give you an exception.

No, exceptions apart, to save large sums of money you must handle large sums of money. Very well, how do those who handle and gather and live on and leave large sums of money come by it?

Ah! You can always learn how a man leaves his money, but it is very seldom you hear how he came by it. We have laws against fortune-telling for the future. I wish we had laws for more fortune-telling in respect of the past.

I suppose we should find, if all secrets were revealed to us, that some of the great family fortunes go back to the dark ages, or at any rate to the dim ages, when such of the great landed and titled families as are still in existence and remain wealthy got their domains and their titles to revenues; but I doubt if they amount to much in the sum total of current private wealth.

Some others no doubt go back to that ability remarked upon by the Prince of Denmark—the ability to "crook the pregnant hinges of the knee, where thrift may follow fawning." Some others doubtless date back to nothing more meritorious than a lucky fluke. There has been more good luck than good management in many a bouncing career. Some others have been extorted by holding up and levying toll upon the industrious public—highwayman fashion.

I think we should find, however, that the bulk of owned and inherited money has been made, and is being made, in business: some of it, of course, in shady business; some of it even in downright dirty business; but by far the greater part of it in good honest business by people of exceptional qualities who have given the public, out of whom all fortunes are made, value for money. By "business" I mean every manner of creative and constructive and productive contriving and organizing and managing of human affairs.

A working man came and walked beside me as I left a lecture hall a few months ago. I had been talking about wealth and poverty. He was one of those who think things over for themselves. He said: "What puzzles me, Mr. Hilton, is this. What have I ever done, or what has my lot ever done, towards inventing or planning all those things we have nowadays at our beck and call. Who invented the 'bus I ride on or the radio I listen to or anything else? Not me. Not my sort. Then who are we to grudge profits or big incomes to the clever ones? Without them we should be still in our mud huts. What's the answer to that, Mr. Hilton?" I hope I gave him a convincing answer. He didn't look very convinced.

To save big money you must make big money, and to make big money you must either get a strangle-hold on the public; or you must invent, or organize, or direct, or trade, or exploit; or you must get into a highly paid profession; or you must develop some rare faculty that has a high market price. Then you can make your hundreds and put your fifties by. You can make your thousands and put your hundreds by—with ever-increasing ease and security; with ever-gathering momentum. That you must do; and only by so doing, with the rarest exceptions, can you become the man who dies worth £100,000, or the man who leaves £2,000,000.

"With ever-increasing ease and security, and with ever-gathering momentum." Is that true? Does money make money and do riches pave the way to still more easily acquired riches? Is the first thousand the hardest of the thousands, the first million the hardest of the millions? If it is true, is it more true than it used to be—or less? And is money getting harder and harder to lose?

If it be true that in these days more than ever money makes money and money made by money stays put, then we may already have the reason, or a good deal of it, why in spite of all the heavy taxation of big incomes and big estates the shape of the wealth pyramid remains virtually unchanged.

"Clogs to clogs in three generations," my Lancashire forbears used to say. In those early days of the Industrial Revolution there was truth in it. Men ventured the fortunes they had made. They competed fiercely, and as their businesses went up and down so did their private substance. Not so now. There are lands in which you can find the ex-magnate in the bread line. The ballads at any rate tell of his presence there. But we had a saying for him, too. It was "Up like a rocket, down like a stick."

Even here in England you can come across the one-time man of means in St. Martin's Crypt or on the Embankment. Don't expect to find him in the first ten. Have patience. Be reasonable. You'll find him in the first hundred, belike. You might even find, not in the first hundred, but in the first thousand, a man of "family." Such things have happened. But, apart from the rarest personal disasters and tragedies, "family" in our land stays put. Wealth stays put. Riches to-day have a high margin of safety.

So the personnel of the wealth pyramid becomes almost congealed on its several planes. There are notable exceptions. They stand out in your thoughts just because they are exceptions. But the rule is— born of a squire, be a squire; born of a labourer, be a labourer; born of a magnate, be a magnate.

As the wealth is, so is the schooling; as the schooling is, so is the appointment; as the appointment is, so is the income to be expected and conceded. There are exceptions. They are for ever being quoted. The rule remains the rule.

Yes, the income. But why should that apply to the possessions? It may be true that those of the low-wage classes who save £5,000 are as rare as blood-allies; but surely it needn't be true. Surely it needn't.

Look what anyone can do by persistent and systematic saving. Provided your income is nicely above bare subsistence level, all you need do to accumulate a pretty fortune is start young, tell someone to keep back one-tenth of your earnings, put that one-tenth away at compound interest in a safe place, adjust your manner of living accordingly (you'll never miss what you've never had); and in half or three-quarter a lifetime you'll be a man of means.

If you'll pass it on, when you die, to the son and daughter, and they start where you left off and follow your thrifty ways . . . why, at the end of a couple of generations—provided by then a fool or a wastrel hasn't been born to the family, and no one's gone into business and failed, and there's been no war and inflation to melt it away—there'll be two more families of means in the land, especially if the young lady and the young fellow your son and daughter marry have also come into a little sum from their parents.

For consider what small sums steadily accumulated can amount to. Five shillings a week put by at 3 per cent interest will in forty years amount to £1,000. Seven and six a week for forty years would accumulate precisely that sum I named as the average per family if the total wealth of the country were evenly spread. Or if you'll envisage three generations, extending over a period of say seventy years, then even 1s. 6d. a week steadily withheld from expenditure and accumulated at 3 per cent means at the end of the period £1,000. Even 1s. 6d. a week! If you make it 5s. a week it would amount, in the three-generation period, to £3,300 per family!

"That's all very well," you may say, "but five shillings, and still more seven and six, is a lot of money. How many families could set aside so much without starving body, mind, or spirit?"

Well, it is true that a good many could not. It is said that at least 20 per cent of our population in 1938 is living near or below the threshold of adequate nutrition. With these, there is no margin for saving. Their incomes, when you allow for necessary expenses of other kinds, afford them only just enough or in some cases nothing like enough to buy proper food. It is true, of course, that in real life nearly all these families find something from their meagre incomes for indulgences. But who wouldn't? Think of the lives they lead, in such surroundings, and in such gloom of spirit and outlook. Even so, they do it by stinting themselves the necessities of life.

All that is shamefully true of some million or two

of our families. To expect saving of them, except saving in pence that they may accumulate a few shillings for the cheap boots and the overcoat and the bargain bedding (and I hope the occasional tiny beano) which they could otherwise never command at all, or could only command by signing on the dotted line and paying through the nose, would be to expect a vain thing.

They are all too numerous, these families below saving level. I shall be saying a good deal more about them in the next chapter; but if it be true that 20 per cent of our families in 1938 are below the saving-possibility mark it follows, unless my arithmetic is at fault, that there were 80 per cent on or above that level; that is to say, 80 per cent who, by living a little below their incomes, could steadily accumulate through the years.

Among that 80 per cent the "working-class family" must be heavily represented. I am always a little hazy as to what precisely is a working-class family, and have on many an occasion, official and otherwise, evaded defining it; but I am told by those who say they know that of our twelve million families nearly ten million are "working-class."

If that be so, then there is a great centre group of working-class people, some of whom do save, and all of whom could save if they wanted to: all of whom could become, by saving, the rightful owners of three-quarters of the ownable wealth of our land instead of the miserable fragment of it which is their share at present.

All they need do, to become stockholders in the nation instead of propertyless hirelings and retainers, is this. If their wages are 65s., live at the rate of 60s. If their wages are £5 a week, live at the rate of £4 10s. Simple as falling off a stool! Hats off to self-helpful Samuel Smiles!

But come, isn't this precisely what they are in fact doing! Did I not end my last chapter with a reference to the "£3,000 million of Small Savings," which, as the newspapers said, is "£300 in the locker for each working-class family"? I'll now go even further, and remark that the £3,000,000,000 shows an increase of £700,000,000 in only four years between 1934 and 1938, and every year brings a further stupendous addition. So, if these totals mean anything to our purpose, the process of common folk acquiring a bumper share in the wealth of the land is going on apace and we need do nothing but let well alone. Evidently we must look at this table of Small Savings with its total of £3,000,000,000.

First, then, let me say that £3,000,000,000, though it looks a lot, is only one-seventh of the total privately owned wealth of the country. Even if that amount really should prove, to the utter confounding of Daniels and Campion, to be widely dispersed among our populace, giving £300 per family, there would still be the other six-sevenths of the privately ownable wealth in other hands.

None the less it is a substantial and important sum, and wants looking into; especially as, if you allow for those who are within the range of public assistance and unemployment assistance and so on, who quite positively and demonstrably have nothing at all in hand, it must arithmetically follow that the typical self-supporting wage-earning or small-salary-earning family must have a thousand or two put by.

So we had better look at the items. They can be seen in the table on page 58. It is the table annually calculated by well-meaning unofficial persons and annually quoted, with governmental blessing, by responsible Ministers in the House of Commons.

Let us keep to round figures. There are £500 millions in National Savings Certificates; there are nearly £700 millions in the Post Office; and there are £250 millions in Trustee and Municipal Savings Banks.

Those three lots make nearly £1,500 millions; and it is all in institutions actually designed and created to cater for the small investor.

But at once comes the crucial question. It is this. How far are the depositors in truth persons of small means, and how far are they persons of ample means who have chosen to put away small parcels of their wealth in one or more (perhaps all) of these institutions?

Here is mystery indeed, worthy of a Committee consisting of Colonel Anthony Gethryn, Monsieur Poirot, Charlie Chan, and Inspector Hornleigh: with, of course, Lord Peter Wimsey in the Chair. We can only do our poor, uninspired best. Where shall we look for a clue?

I have had valued help from the Post Office authorities, and the Secretary of the National Savings Committee, and the Trustee Savings

SMALL SAVINGS (*In millions of pounds*)

	1934 £	1938 £
National Savings Certificates ...	480	517·1
Post Office Savings Bank	331	498·6
Trustee Savings Banks	172	234·3
Birmingham Municipal Bank ...	15	23·8
Post Office Register	224	203·0
Building Societies	464	695·0
Industrial and Provident Societies	182	261·0
Industrial Assurance	300	385·1
Friendly Societies	126	137·0
National Health Insurance Funds ...	127½	136·4
Superannuation, etc., Trust Funds	41½	65·7
Trade Unions	11½	16·4
Railway Savings Banks	17½	25·4
	£2,492	£3,198·8

Note : These figures do *not* include

> (*a*) Ordinary life assurance.
> (*b*) Ownership of own house.
> (*c*) Holdings of "small savers" in commercial banks, railways, and other joint-stock enterprises.
> (*d*) Capital invested in small businesses.
> (*e*) Household goods and chattels.

Banks. I am grateful for all this. They put at my disposal such data as they could from which I might gather what sort of people they are who have accounts and how much they have on deposit.

As to the sort of people they are; that is easily

answered. The vast majority of those who use the Post Office and Trustee Savings Banks are persons of small incomes and probably of small means; among them a certain number of children. This great majority has savings of a few shillings or a pound or two.

But now one wants to know how the grand total of deposits is distributed among the whole number. Ah, that is more difficult. The *average* deposit of the 11,000,000 people who use the Post Office Savings Bank is round about £60. The average for those who use the Trustee Savings Banks is about the same. Where does this mighty average come from, when multitudes have only a few shillings to their name?

Why, of course, it comes from a few people depositing pretty large sums. You will probably know that you mustn't put into the Post Office more than £500 in any one year. But don't get a wrong idea from that. If one in ten deposit a few hundreds—perhaps from the sale of a business, or a matured endowment policy, or a burial insurance payment—you will easily get a £60 average even though the other nine-tenths have deposited no more than a few shillings.

Averages here hide more than they reveal. What we need is what the statisticians call a dispersion. You must know how many of those who bank with the savings banks have so much to their credit, how many have so much, and how many so much, right up the scale to those, if there are any, who have thought it wise to put £20,000 of their £200,000 fortune into "Small Savings."

Let me make a suggestion which I hope will commend itself to the Savings Bank Authorities. It is that they should take, on any random basis, one in a thousand of their accounts and analyse them as a representative sample of the whole. In the case of the Post Office it would give 11,000 accounts. The results from that 11,000 would represent with only the most minute degree of error the position in regard to the whole of their clientèle. It would, I think, throw light on the savings position which would not only be useful to those who have to study these matters, but would also be of value in matters of administration and policy.

Pending that, all I can offer is the following tabulation relating to the end of 1934 when a section of Post Office accounts was examined. It was found that:

(a) In 70 per cent of the accounts the balance was less than £25, the average being £4 1s.

(b) In 16·5 per cent of the accounts the balance was between £25 and £100, the average being £53.

(c) In 13·5 per cent of the accounts the balance was over £100.

Here the true shapes begin to loom through the haze. Even in the Post Office seven out of ten of the depositors have only a small amount to their credit,

ranging from a few shillings in the general case to
£25 in the rare case and averaging (O average,
what errors are committed in thy name!) only £4.
Eight out of ten have less than £100.

I am not finding fault with that. It is what the
Post Office Savings Bank is for. It is doing its job,
and doing it well. But it is idle to quote the Post
Office in disproof of the statement that only four
million of our families are worth as much as £100,
that four million are worth from a pound or two up
to a hundred, and that four million have nothing
but what they stand up in or sit down at—if
that.

"In 13·5 per cent of the accounts the balance was
over £100." You would notice perhaps that though
I could give you an average for the other categories
I could not for this. I do not know what the average
holding of this 13·5 per cent of the larger depositors
is, nor do I know its dispersion within the average.
It can be inferred from the figures that the average
for these relative few must be some hundreds of
pounds. But even that statement may mask a large
number of deposits of a hundred or two and a very
few deposits of much larger amounts.

The eleven million, then, with "money in the
Post Office" are mostly persons with very small
deposits—of a shilling to a pound or two. The persons with really substantial amounts in the Post
Office are relatively few in number and their
holdings form the bulk of the total. There is nothing
here to challenge the picture I have drawn of our

national wealth-distribution. Indeed, it fits perfectly into my pattern.

Now if this be true of the Post Office, it certainly applies quite as much to the Trustee and Municipal Savings Banks with their £250,000,000 total deposits and to the holding of the £500,000,000 of National Savings Certificates in 1938. I do not think I need here make any analysis of them. It would only show, even more than the Post Office figures, that the substantial savers are a smallish group of the populace.

The Trustee Savings Banks, as you probably know, are managed by local Committees of Trustees, who may receive no payment for their services. The object of the Banks is to provide a safe place for savings and a full banking service to the "small man." There are no shareholders and no "profits" are aimed at or distributed. Surpluses on working remain in the Bank funds for the benefit of depositors. No sum is too small for the Bank—facilities are available, with them as with the Post Office, and indeed with the Joint Stock Banks, for saving in pennies, e.g. by stamp cards or by Home Safes.

I think it is true to say that the officers in attendance at the Trustee Savings Banks are much more in the nature of guide, counsellor, and friend to the client than the Post Office official or local postmaster can possibly be. They claim to know, and I am sure they do know, a great deal about their depositors.

Now and then, here and there, I talk with them— the managers and actuaries of the Trustee Savings

Banks. Excellent and knowledgeable men they are, but invariably they hold the view that the typical family is one with a good round sum laid by: a few hundred pounds or so. They try not to smile when they hear of the Campion analysis; but if only I or Mr. Campion knew what they know, could see with their eyes and hear with their ears the real truth about the working classes instead of playing about with probate figures and doing statistical exercises which end in obvious nonsense, how much wiser we should be!

I understand this attitude of theirs; but it is they who are wrong. They think their clients, and especially the ones who come in most often, are typical. Aren't they always seeing them! Their impressions, with all respect to them, are worthless —I mean as affording a picture of the nation as a whole. Their members are, could they but grasp the nation, mere bright spots in an otherwise rather drab national pattern. But they cannot see it. They have no eye, you will find, for the multitudes who do not come through their swing doors.

Wait a moment, though. Suppose a good many of those with quite small accounts at one or other of these institutions have a bit of money in several! Then where are you?

I cannot tell you. No one can. All I can say is this. To my mind it is unlikely that the very small saver in one office has a duplicate savings account in another. It is much more likely that the person with the big deposit in one has a big or small deposit in another. Whatever the uneven dispersion of holdings may be in any one of these institutions, it is likely to be much more uneven if you could take them all together—lumping the balances of clients using two or more. If you say that a good many folk have a bit in all three, then you have knocked yet another chip off the £3,000,000,000 image of the small saver.

That portion of the "Small Savings" total at which I have so far looked amounted to one-half of the whole. Let me take a brief glance at the items that make up the rest.

A substantial further item is the £700,000,000 of share capital and deposits in Building Societies. I will not bother to analyse the dispersion of this amount among the investors and holders. Much more than in the case of Savings Banks they are likely to be persons of comfortable or ample means.

Then there is the £270,000,000 of the Industrial and Provident Societies. These are for the most part the Co-operative Societies and the various clubs. The total includes, I find, surplus funds and certain liabilities other than share capital and deposits so that the amount of personally withdrawable, holdings may be not more than £150,000,000. That amount is likely to be held in less unequal parcels than the Building Society money; but it will not be very different from the Post Office holding.

Then there is the £380,000,000 of funds accumulated by the Industrial Assurance Companies, which are in the main the companies engaged in

Burial Insurance (with a relatively very little Endowment Insurance) and who collect the premiums by house-to-house visits. But surely that £380,000,000 has no place here. That is the gross sum in hand. But (except for endowment policies—a trifling proportion of the whole) the saver cannot touch what stands in his name except in a specified contingency—generally death.

These Sums in Hand do not "belong" to the savers. At most the total to be regarded as "savings" is the amount contributors would receive if they all wanted to surrender their policies and if they were to be given an equitable surrender value for them. That sum is not more than half, perhaps not one-third or one-quarter, of £380,000,000. The rest belongs to the companies.

Never in any circumstances will it reach the insured persons. Indeed, not until the end of the world—the world as we know it—is in sight will that amount conceivably be allowed to shrink. Then how can it be said to "belong" to the small saver? Certainly there are "savings" here, and they are widely dispersed "savings." There is matter for satisfaction in their magnitude and in their growth. But the realizable portion of them does not, all told, loom large in the aggregate of Small Savings. There is nothing in the Industrial Assurance figures to cast doubt upon the picture I have drawn.

And then, if you are going to take the Industrial Assurance balances, why don't you take the £136 million included as "Accumulated Funds under the National Health Insurance Acts"? Because if you do you will see at once that you are playing with a meaningless figure. A bad spell, and the fund might fall to zero. That might occasion some slight modification of contributions and benefits, but it would leave the position of persons insured under the Health and Pensions Scheme much the same. The tremendous transactions of National Health and Pensions Insurance and the huge capital value of the titles to eventual benefits bear no sort of relation to cash in hand. The size of the accumulated funds is an irrelevance, and has no place in this table.

I will not go into the make-up of the Superannuation Funds (£65·7 million), the Trade Union Funds (£16·4 million), or the Industrial Savings Banks Balances (Railway, £25·4 millions). Important as they are, their totals regarded as savings are relatively small; and their dispersion is not likely to differ much from that of the Post Office and Trustee Banks.

So, when I examined the figures for the Post Office and Trustee and Municipal Savings Banks, I examined that half of the total least favourable to my pattern. The pattern remains. The alleged £3,000,000,000 of Small Savings quoted for the year 1938 is a figment of fancy. The "Savings" are all right. It is the "Small" that is meaningless.

It provides an odd commentary upon the mistiness that shrouds all these vastly important matters, and the confusions of mind that prevail in respect of them, that the conventional total of £3,000,000,000 with which I have been dealing and which I have shown to contain various inadmissible items, includes nothing for houses owned by the people living in them, or for the cottage or the row of cottages from which some not at all well-to-do persons draw rents on which, after paying the charges, they contrive to live. Shadowy figures have been included; but solid house figures have been omitted. Why?

Why, because we know even less as to who owns what in the sphere of house-ownership than in any other wealth-ownership sphere. From no official source, from no source whatsoever, can you get trustworthy information as to how the house-property of Great Britain is held and as to how far the titular ownership must be discounted by reason of mortgages.

One of the marvels of our time has been the growth in the building societies. In ten years their business has nearly trebled. In 1938 the 1,000 societies had 2,000,000 share investors and 800,000 depositors, lending money to 1,400,000 persons to assist them in acquiring dwelling houses and business property for occupation and for investment. Members' subscriptions to the share capital are accumulated in a fund which may be augmented by deposits and loans. Advances are made from that fund to assist members in the purchase of properties. Security for advances is given by a mortgage upon the property purchased. Re-payments are spread over 15, 20 or 25 years. The amount involved, as I have said, is over £700,000,000 (Shares £520,000,000; Deposits, £140,000,000; Loans, Profit and Reserve, £54,000,000).

This immense and ever-growing activity ought to denote, one would think, millions of families who either own outright the house they live in or who have purchased and are paying for it through a building society on the instalment plan with the house as security for the loan on the purchase money. Is that the case? Or is it not?

No one knows. It seems to be no one's business to know. The only partial—very partial—sidelight on the question comes from a private research organization—the British Institute of Public Opinion. That Institute (of American inspiration by the way) takes chosen cross-sections of the population of Great Britain by methods which give a small sample selected so as to be representative of the public at large. By these enquiries of the tiniest of samples it obtains results which must seem to those unacquainted with Enquiry by Sample miraculously accurate.

Recently the Institute asked its interviewers to find out what was the proportion of home-owners in the sample cross-section of the population used in its latest survey. Home-owners note: not house-owners.

The interviewers found that of those questioned:

15 per cent owned their homes.

9 per cent were buying their homes.

76 per cent paid rent for their homes.

Those were the all-over results. Of course, the degree of home-owning varied with the income.

Among the well-to-do (over £500 a year) the proportion of home-owners was 53 per cent, with 11 per cent in the process of becoming home-owners. Only 36 per cent of this group paid rent for their living accommodation.

Among the less well-off (£200 to £500) only 19 per cent owned their homes, but 13 per cent were buying them, whereas some 68 per cent paid rent.

Among the poorer families (£200 and less) the proportion of rent payers rose to 90 per cent. Home-owners and home-buyers only made up 5 per cent each of those questioned in that group.

Now this is extraordinarily valuable information; and we must be grateful for it. At the same time it should be noted that it does not tell us, and we do not know, what the values of the houses were. It does not tell us how many of the houses "owned" were mortgaged, and to what proportion of their value. It does not tell us what part of the value of the house under purchase had been paid. And, of course, it does not tell us anything about the owner-ship of houses other than the one occupied.

Nor is there anything in the conventional total about goods and chattels. The reason is that we know next to nothing about it. We know next to nothing about household goods and gear (below the probate limit) except that, proud as their owners may be of them, and rightly proud, and much as they may have cost in the first instance, (*a*) they are not available as savings to be drawn on in an emergency, (*b*) they ought not to be pledged as security for loans, and (*c*) they would not, if sold, realize in the typical case more than a very small sum in the auction room.

We know that even on estates of a gross value between £100 and £300 the value of the household goods is normally assessed at an average of only £11, and that the value of household goods represents only one-twentieth of the value of the estates.

I have led you through these rather tedious figures lest I should have them thrown at me from every side at every step. But nothing has come out of any of them, or out of all of them put together, concerning the distribution of wealth ownership in this country that can call in question, or even supplement, the conclusions reached by Daniels and Campion from their analysis of the probate figures.

Many attempts have been made to distil from the gross total of Small Savings a sum representing the aggregate holdings of the real "small saver." Much zeal and much labour has gone in such arithmetic alchemy.

One searcher among the data comes to the conclusion that the true figure of Savings by Small Savers, whom he takes as persons of £400 a year and under, is £2,750,000,000 (Mr. H. Oliver Horne, Actuary of the Aberdeen Savings Bank, in his pamphlet *The Assets of the Small Saver*, May 1937) which he says "represents some £65 for each small saver, including house property, furniture, cash, and every sort of realizable asset."

Another expert (Mr. Douglas Jay, City Editor of the *Daily Herald*, November 1937) is uneasy at the £400 a year. He feels we ought to know how much of the £3,000,000,000 is owned by the "working class." He rejects £400 a year in favour of an upper limit of £5 a week. He thereupon gets a figure of £1,500,000,000 for the savings of those under £5 a week, and he thinks the average saving is £135 per family. But if real property and industrial assurance are included the right figure, he says, is £195 per family.

I ventured to tell a labourer friend of mine working on a building site that according to expert opinion he and his mates possessed an average family fortune of £195. His comment was expressive, and, I think, illuminating. He said: "Gaw-blimey!"

All these analyses are completely worthless, as I have shown. You can analyse the figures till doomsday; you can turn loose on them the most accomplished statisticians in the world: and you will still get nothing out of them that will tell you the distribution of privately ownable property in our country. Nothing whatsoever. The figures cannot in their nature yield the information you want. You cannot produce the rabbit of wealth distribution out of any one of those hats, and the more you put the hats together the greater becomes the confusion and the more the rabbit eludes your grasp

and peeps at you or frisks his tail from behind
six hats at once.

I wish I could hope that what I have said above
will put an end to the story of the Small Saver and
his £3,000,000,000 and to the talk of the typical
working-class family with its £300 in the bank. But
nonsense dies hard, and I am not sanguine.

To know the facts of working-class or any other
class savings and debts you must go to the house.
There is no other way. Now the only people who go
to the house to ask questions, when it is appropriate
they should, are the revenue officers, the Public
Assistance officers, the Unemployment Assistance
Board officers, and social welfare visitors of one kind
or another. I have already dealt with the first three.
I have shown how, taken together, they bear out
my guess, based on Campion, of four million families
with £100 or more, four million with anything from
a pound or two up to £100, and four million living
from hand to mouth with nothing but what they
stand up in—if that; and many of them at or near
destitution. What I have not yet examined is the
possibility of obtaining inside knowledge of the
ownings and owings of the poorest of the poor.
That is for my next chapter.

To end this section on the "Small Saver," let me
say how lamentable it is that there should be this
almost complete absence of direct data regarding
the ownings and the owings of those worth less
than £100. Is it that we would rather not know?
If so, I think we ought to be made to know. There-

fore I make a suggestion. It is that probate officers, instead of taking no further interest in estates of deceased persons once they are satisfied that the net possessions do not amount to as much as £100, should record such facts as they can discover regarding the possessions and the debts of *all* who die.

It need not be done on anything like so elaborate a scale as in the case of the estates upon which estate duty is to be levied, and the information to be recorded would be trifling by comparison with that which has to be done on the estates of the better-off.

If revenue officers could be instructed by Parliament to add this to their other duties, and if the Inland Revenue Department would present us with an analysis of the estates under £100, just as it does of those over £100, we could by applying the methods of Daniels and Campion deduce from the complete tabulation truths about the distribution of wealth among our populace, which would be of the utmost value in judging the nature of the common weal and in shaping public policy relative thereto.

Only the probate officer has the right to ask these questions of all and sundry. Only he is expert at learning and recording the truth. There is no reason in public policy or in respect for privacy or in consideration for relatives' feelings why he should lose interest at the £100 point. There is every reason why he should treat all alike so far as obtaining and recording information goes.

If the work involved in obtaining "information for its own sake" should be deemed too great and too costly, then let the particulars be taken of one in ten; or, if even that be expense unwarrantable since all it would yield would be information about people from whom no revenue was going to be obtained, let the procedure be confined to those whose deaths were accidentally caused. That would yield information as to about one in thirty of all estates at death, a total of 18,000 per annum. The very nature of the cause of death would have the effect (here speaks the statistician in whom professional detachment can subsist along with compassion!) of giving a sample well-spread over the age-groups, relatively unbiased by long illness and poor physical endowment, and therefore perfect for the purpose I have in mind.

Let what I have said in this chapter not be misunderstood. I would not have it supposed for one moment that I am making light of the magnificent work of our Savings institutions. On the contrary. I am full of admiration for it, regard it as second to none in national importance and desire to see it advance by leaps and bounds. I have had many personal contacts in late years with the officers of the National Savings Committee and with voluntary workers in the Savings Movement. It is my desire to further their aims and activities to the utmost of my power. What I have been saying has for one of its implications the immense field for expansion that still lies open to Savings activity.

CHAPTER III

WHY ARE THE POOR POOR?

I WAS talking the other day with a hard-headed man of affairs. I was saying it was odd that in a country of ever-increasing affluence like this of ours there should be four million families worth all told not more than somewhere between a pound or two and a hundred pounds, and another four million families living from hand to mouth with nothing in the world but what they stand up in and sit down to—and many of them not that, since they are chronically or fitfully in debt. He said: "Well, what d'you expect? You know what people are!"

Is *that* it, then? Is *that* why so few own so much and so many own next to nothing or less than nothing? Is it that the rich are rich because they are a rich sort and the poor are poor because they are a poor sort—and the in-betweens are in-between because they are a medium sort, and everyone is pretty much where you would expect one of that sort to be—and pretty much where he ought to be?

If so, there's nothing to bother about except to see that the rich sort don't make too much of a nuisance of themselves with their blessed riches and the poor sort don't make too much of a nuisance of themselves with their cursed poverty.

And, after all, isn't there a lot to be said for that point of view? Don't we know, all of us, that in any largish family gathering there'll be the one who never seems to make headway at anything: perhaps because he's not very bright, you know; or because he's never been strong, poor lad; or because he *will* cut a dash without asking where the money's to come from; or because he was born with a hole in his pocket; or because . . . oh, well, because he's that sort. He's had bestowed on him from infancy the collective good advice and admonishment of the whole tribe of his relatives—to say nothing of wise counsel from teachers and pastors and masters—and nothing's ever altered him and ever will. He's that sort.

Then why fuss about there being among the populace generally lots and lots who've never got on and are for ever in a hole? Isn't it natural? Wasn't it once said: "The poor ye have always with you"? Isn't that true? And isn't it because there are always among us people who were stamped "poor" the day they were born? That sort—and always will be?

It seemed to me, quite early on, that we should have to look carefully into this; so I cast about for up-to-date information on what sort of folk the very poor are, and whether it is true that in the main they are poor just because they are a poor sort. It will now come as no surprise to anyone that I could find next to nothing dealing directly with why the poor are poor. Masses of data on this and that. Stacks of dogma by economic politicians who know all about it without any looking or pondering. But

nothing to throw much light on the simple question:
Why is this and that poor family poor?

So off I went to Ben Astbury, of the Charity
Organisation Society. I was a little doubtful, and a
little afraid. I was prepared to be told that he was
weary of explaining the obvious to day trippers like
myself. But not at all. On the contrary. He said he
himself and those who worked with him had long
wanted to gather up their knowledge and ideas of
these things and to come to grips with the very
problems that were in my mind. So far from merely
allowing himself to be persuaded to help me: he
threw himself with enthusiasm into giving me every
possible aid in the search for an answer to my conun-
drum.

He wrote off to all Secretaries of the Charity
Organisation Society in the London area asking
them each to take about ten families from among
those with whom they were in touch, ten fairly
typical or representative families, and set down the
story of each one, with special attention to certain
points which Mr. Astbury and I concocted between
us. At the same time he wrote to a number of his
friends engaged in similar social work in the provinces
asking if they also would collaborate.

They responded nobly; and in due course there
reached me the stories of three hundred and more
poor families in all parts of the kingdom: in the
cotton, steel, coal, and shipping centres; in one or
two seaside towns; in an ancient cathedral city; in a
village or two; and in housing estates on the skirts

of large industrial areas. Many of those furnishing the information also gave their personal views, derived from a long and wide experience of these matters, upon the issues raised.

Three hundred propertyless households. A tiny sample, I know. Still, one answering much of my purpose. At any rate, they were something—and in these matters something is always better than nothing. I set to work to distil from them whatever they might yield of the essence of the problem before me.

The statistical analyses were done for me by my Cambridge colleague, Mr. E. Rothbarth. I tender him my grateful thanks. With his deductions before me I was able to get much more surely the pattern, as well as the sense and feel, of the material sent in by Mr. Astbury's associates. I met many of these gifted people in conference, and had the opportunity of discussing outstanding points with them in person.

Be clear about these families of whom I shall now speak. They are *not* typical working-class families. On the contrary, they are quite non-typical of the bulk of our working class, who for the most part do themselves pretty well—either by absolute or by comparative standards. Not as well as they might, no doubt. But pretty well.

They are, and are typical of, that lower tenth (or lower fifth if you think that a truer fraction) of our working-class families who at any given time do not know how to make ends meet and who are, for long spells or for the time being, on the brink

or in the abyss of under-nourishment and penury
and debt. You must remember that these are each
and all families who in their distress of mind or body
or estate have sought charitable aid or have had
charitable aid applied for on their behalf. Only so
have they and their circumstances come to the
knowledge of those who have given me their stories.

Very well. Here they are, the three hundred and
more stories of families in poverty and distress. We
want to know whether they are poor because they
are that sort; or whether they are poor because they
haven't had a square deal. We want to know why
they are as they are.

You shall have the analyses; but it is no use
looking at analyses or reflecting upon generalities
until you have got in your bones and blood the feel
of the living persons with whom they're concerned.
So I shall proceed by way of giving you one and
another of the stories pretty much as they came to
me. I have trimmed a little, but not altered. The
generalizations based on the analyses can be arrived
at as we ponder the stories.

Where shall I start? Perhaps with two of the
families who appear on the face of it to belong to
those who seem to be at the bottom because they
are that sort, and for no other reason.

Here, then, is a youngish tram-driver and his
wife. One child. The husband always in regular
work. A steady wage of £3 4s. a week. You'd have
thought they'd have been in clover. (Many an
unemployed man if he could land such a job would

think himself in paradise.) But not a bit of it. Listen to this:

"Neither the husband nor wife ever had the slightest idea of good management. When they were first in touch with us we found the entire weekly income was being absorbed in the payment of hire purchase, tallymen, money-lenders, and debts; with the result that each week more debts accumulated. We persuaded the different firms concerned to stay their hand in order that we might gradually clear the debts, as we realized that neither the husband nor wife would ever get straight on their own. This plan would have been successful but for the complete lack of co-operation on their part. After many months we realized that they must be left to their own devices. They continue to get into debt and receive many summonses. They are heading for a crash and nothing will stay them. So far as we know they had no vices other than a little mild gambling."

There you have the thriftless and shiftless. Nothing to do with social injustice. Nothing to do with unemployment. Spendthrift born or spendthrift made. Not wastrels but wasters. Muddlers and fritterers. Friends can do nothing with them. Skilled and sympathetic would-be helpers can do nothing with them. Then what *is* to be done with them except let them be what nature made them? Face that, and answer it.

One other of the same type to impress the picture

on our minds. A young man in the early thirties and his wife. He is a specialist craftsman. Was earning £5 a week. Never knew unemployment. The wife has a small inheritance, an annuity of £1 a week. They have four children, the eldest aged 8. The family health is good enough. Here, too, you would have thought, were all the conditions for a happy and prospering home. But now hear:

"Neither the man nor his wife have any idea of money matters. The wife is said to be the chief offender. At one time they got so badly into debt, to the extent of over £200, that the man's firm had to come to the rescue, deducting afterwards so much from his wages towards repayment. Despite the firm's efforts the wife still continued to get further into debt. It was plain she had not realized the position in the very least.

"The man then began to stay away from his employment because he said he felt so ashamed, and was finally dismissed. Since that time he has been unemployed on and off. They still continue to get into debt wherever they go. The relatives, some of whom are in very good positions, have done their utmost, and are in despair as to what steps should be taken next.

"Neither of them drinks or gambles, apart from an odd sixpence a week on pools. They appear devoted to the children. They both make a very good impression and are well educated, but they are quite incapable of managing their finances."

Let those two serve for the hundreds of thousands of thriftless and shiftless by birth or by upbringing. What is to be done with them? What is to be done *about* them?

Perhaps nothing. Perhaps all one can do is to let them stew in their own juice. But at any rate we can ask whether we can slow down the production of their sort. So far as it is a matter of breeding we need not expect quick results. But how far is it rather a matter of teaching and training? Still more how far is it a matter of the ideals and values of our age being a little on the shoddy and the tinsel side? How far have they just taken colour from the thought and chatter and life of our time?

We ought not to take it, I think, that even these were foredoomed to be what they are on the day they made their appearance in the world. Not altogether. Surely we can envisage a social and educational order in which not so many grew up thriftless and shiftless. There will always be some; but there need not always be as many as now.

But for the present there they are, in their hundreds of thousands, in every walk of life and every grade of society. The shiftless and the thriftless. Eat, drink, and be merry or miserable; and hope the bailiffs will not come for quite a long time. Never mind whom you bilk and defraud. Dodge your way through life and don't give a hang for anyone.

The shiftless and the thriftless. It does not seem to matter very much whether the income is two, ten or twenty pounds a week—they will spend as they go, they will overspend; be always in debt, never in funds.

What to do about them may not be very clear. But this is certain. Any theorizing we may start as to why the rich are rich and the poor are poor had better take them into account. Economic theory that is not based on a knowledge of *people* is economic rubbish.

Of course, if they have great possessions well safeguarded they can waste and still carry on. But if they have small or no possessions they will be, whatever you do, down in the bottomest layer of your four million families who own nothing but pawntickets and debts. And they will be there, not because of the mechanism of society, but because they are what they are.

While we are still on persons, and the natures with which they were born or reared, perhaps I had better pick out one or two who may perhaps be where they are because they have some kink that gets them into trouble with law-abiding and law-enforcing society. A touch of dishonesty, perhaps, practised on too small a scale and clumsily; or a streak of brutality or sexual oddity. They get into trouble, are denounced, arrested, sentenced, and go to gaol. Thereafter they find it difficult to get back into steady employment at a living wage.

You shall have just two which tell of a criminal record. Here are man and wife aged about 40. There are four children. They married soon after he

left the army in 1921. He hasn't had much regular
work through all those years—but enough to qualify
him for Unemployment Assistance. He is a strong
and healthy ruffian. The wife is a sick and beaten
woman. The children are undernourished and
ailing. They get free milk at school and cod-liver
oil and malt from charitable funds. Indeed, the
whole family lives and looks like living mostly at
public charge. The total family income is 47s. a
week. Now listen:

> "This home shows a really dreadful state of
> affairs. The wife's ill health is almost entirely the
> husband's fault. We sent her to a convalescent
> home. A fortnight away from her husband trans-
> formed her; but he insisted on her coming home
> and almost immediately she was the brutalized
> drab once more. He drinks pretty heavily. He
> has had numerous convictions for larceny, false
> pretences, etc."

Well, what of that family? Of course, it may have
been lack of work and opportunity that brutalized
him. Who can say? But in your puzzlings as to why
the poor are poor, don't forget him and his like.
Their name may not be legion, but they count in
the total. Economic theory that ignores the natures
of humans in their infinite variety is economic
balderdash.

Or it may not be a kink so much as a slip; one
that any one of us might make if we got into the
same sort of hopeless tangle. Take this one. A

semi-skilled labourer and his wife. They are in the early thirties. There are four young children. His wages when at work have been 53s. a week, but he has been out of work a good deal. Three years ago he had an injury in a street accident. He was offered a sum by way of compensation but refused it. Against all advice he took a County Court action. He lost: and was landed in £100 of debt for costs, which they are paying off at a shilling or two a week. He is still suffering from the injuries received, and ought to go to hospital to be put right; but dare not lest he be ordered to stop work. He is sick and damaged. The wife's health is poor. Three of the four children are ailing. They took a lodger to help out; but it ended in disaster. Indecent assault—and prison. They are loaded with debts; for some of which he has "been inside." They both drink deep when they have money in hand. I will quote only one phrase of the commentary:

> "This couple married in a mess and have been in a mess ever since. There is no present prospect of their ever getting out."

There you have a whole ragbag of causes: accident, sickness, unemployment, progeny, the kink or the slip, the prison record, litigation, thriftlessness and shiftlessness, and drink when drink can be had. Are they poor because they are that sort or are they poor because they have not had a square deal? Are they victims of a vicious social order or is the poor old social order the aggrieved and injured party? Or is it six of one and half a dozen of the other? Anyhow, what is to be done with them? What is to be done about them? That family is in our four million.

Drink! You would notice those two last mentioned drink. Yet one of my surprises has been how seldom drink occurs as a major item in this tale of abject poverty. A pint here and there in a pail of poverty-causation. No one ever tells the truth about how much he drinks; but these welfare workers get to know things. Even allowing for what they do not get to know, there is surprisingly little drink here. And even so it may be that the misfortune caused the drink rather than the drink caused the misfortune. Who can tell? No doubt, stupefying liquors are playing their part in the impoverishment and degradation of the poorest families, but it is a much smaller part than it used to be; and the one-time belief (I remember it so well) that if it were not for the demon rum the poor would all be healthy, wealthy, and wise is showing itself to be not very well founded.

So some are poor because they are a poor sort. No question of that. The only question is how they came to be a poor sort, and where lies the fault and the blame, and what shall be done to mend matters for the future. For the moment you will be quite content to say, I fancy, that you are not going to sigh because they are without part or lot in the owner-ship of the nation's wealth. You will probably think it not only natural, but a good job. If wealth is to be privately owned, let it be owned by people of better stock and stamina than these.

But equally surely many who are poor are not a poor sort at all—but a right down good sort. The very best sort maybe. These are poor for reasons outside themselves. They've never had a chance, maybe. Or maybe something has come right out of the blue and knocked them endwise, something that was no respecter of persons or of personal worth.

This is quite another matter. How do people of good sort come to be among the poor and wretched? Why did they never get a chance? What are these things that spring upon them unawares and knock the stuffing out of them so that, good as they are, they go down into poverty and cannot, try as they will, struggle back into prosperity again?

The lack of fair chance I will touch on later. It will turn out to be poor parents, poor schooling, early leaving, blind-alley working, low wages, ill surroundings. Excellent material, but never had a chance. Perhaps a large family along with the low wages and the rest. Never had a chance; so had nothing in hand, nothing to fall back upon, when the bolt came from the blue.

What are these bolts from the blue that strike and blast the low-wage family? You won't need to be told the worst two; more damaging than all the rest: unemployment and sickness. In most of my three hundred cases it is one or other of these. Of course, as soon as any poor family has taken a knock from one, the other is soon on the spot to hit it while it is down. If it is sickness that first hits below the belt, unemployment is there in no time to follow up with a little extra punishment. Poverty is no sportsman. It always kicks a man when he is down.

We have already had one glance at sickness; but let us take a simpler case. Here is an oldish man and wife. He's in his early sixties. An engineer's fitter. He was strong and well in his youth, but soon after marriage, long before 1914, he slipped in the street and fractured his spine. He was off work for two years. Ever since he's been plagued with neuritis; but he kept at work until three years ago. Then he had to give up. There is one young daughter. And there is an adult son. It is he who has brought the crowning tragedy to the house. He fell ill with 'flu and bronchitis just as you or I might. But he was very ill; and it led to brain fever. He will never work again. The total family income is 50s. a week, a little of it earned by the daughter, a little from a sick club, the rest from the U.A.B. They waste nothing, squander nothing; except you call a pinch of tobacco and a very occasional sixpence at the pictures waste. They have no outings, not even for a day. They pay 5s. a week into clubs and to a medical association for the sick boy. They won't go one penny into debt.

Well, what about them? Are they poor white trash? It doesn't appear so. They were as sound as you or I. Accident and sickness struck first one, then the other. Hear the visitor's comment:

"A home of almost complete tragedy. Excellent people. His continual hope has been to get back to his work. This, however, is now out of question. Undoubtedly here is a case where there would have been a flourishing and comfortably off family if these disasters had not overtaken them."

Let me give you another "sickness" one. A man and wife in the mid-thirties. Three children of school age and one toddler. He was a miner; strong and hearty and mostly well employed until six years ago, when he caught 'flu, which left him with Graves's disease and neurasthenia. The children start well, but three of them have developed disorders and weaknesses—almost certainly the result of under-nourishment. The family income is 48s. a week; 9s. of it from National Health Insurance, the rest from Public Assistance. No idle money is spent. They are in arrears (£6) with the rent and owe a little here and there, but only a little. All the clothing, bedding, and rugs that could be spared are in pawn; to the total of £5. They got into these straits when the husband first fell ill. They lived then on 18s. a week and pawned rather than ask for relief. He hoped he would get better and start work again. But instead he became incurably ill; and now—there they are. This is what the visitor says of them:

"Here is tragedy indeed. Once I obtained a grant for them to get all their goods out of pawn, but, as you see, they are again all pledged. In spite of the man's ill health they have continued to produce beautiful sound children, who lose their health only when the poverty of the household begins to tell on them."

Are *they* poor because they're a poor sort; made of poor stuff? I do not think so. The crucial blow was struck by 'flu. Does 'flu confine its attentions to the second-rate and the third-rate? Does it permanently damage only the already faulty? I doubt it.

These were excellent people, by all accounts, until sickness struck as impartially as the lightning and crippled the breadwinner, and since they didn't belong to the well-to-do they sank at once to the poverty line. The children, too, now are doomed to ill health and certain poverty.

Now let us see where we are. I am asking why the rich are rich and the comfortable comfortable, and the poor poor. I am asking among other things how it is that four million of our families own nothing or less than nothing of the mighty wealth that fills our land. For the moment I am looking at some of the poorest of that four million. I have looked at the thriftless and shiftless and said you will only get rid of the type by better education, better upbringing, a more wholesome code of social ethics. I have looked at the ones with kinks and records. Now I point to the sick and injured. What are you going to say about them?

Poor stuff? Not at all. It is not a matter of stuff, it's a matter of substance. If you are well-to-do you'll be better seen to. You'll be restored or patched up in better style. You'll be fit and hearty much sooner, even if you convalesce much longer. If you are well-to-do you can carry quite a lot of sickness or accident without tragic waste of substance or failure of means.

Your income may not depend at all on your being able to work. Those who have over £2,000 a year to live on derive more than half of it from investments. One-third of those with £10,000 a year and over draw the whole of their income from investments. In so far as your income is unearned, you can be as ill as you like for as long as you like, your dividend warrants come in just the same. In so far as it is earned, provided your position is sufficiently exalted, you have to be ill a long time before there is any talk of reducing your full pay.

But if you have no substance, no fortune at your back, and if you work for a weekly wage or a small salary, sickness or accident will spell immediate privation and may mean complete disaster. From the ranks of the flourishing artisans or careful clerks whose children are well-fed and well-clothed, and who look to have a little put away as the years go by, you may sink into abject privation and all wretchedness.

Well, is not that just one of life's hazards in a free community? Must you not take that as the sort of thing that must in the nature of things happen? After all, the poor *are* poor and the rich *are* rich. You can't get behind that! And if you are poor, haven't you got to take what comes to you in a sporting you spirit? And if are well off, is it not enough to contribute in your taxes towards the Health Insurance Benefit?—which after all means free doctoring and a small sum each week for six months, and then, if you refuse to get better, the sum is halved for a longish spell before you are told to go on to Public Assistance. And are there not hospitals and charitable institutions and funds galore for very hard cases. Isn't all that pretty good?

Yes, I think it is. Certainly it is worlds better than it used to be. But is it good enough? I see most of these three hundred families haunted and cursed by sickness, and it seems to me plain that we shall not get far with the more equitable distribution of wealth—if that is what we want—until we concentrate vastly more than at present of our social energies and resources upon the restoring of the sick and injured to full health and the preserving of the families of the sick from any and all degradation or even detriment during the work of restoration.

Incapacity caused by accident or by the chance onset of disease is part of the reason why eight of our twelve million families are worth less than £100 all told and why four million of those live from hand to mouth with nothing or less than nothing of personal property to their name. That is the first of the two principal assassins who lurk in the shadows waiting their chance to maltreat and rob the decent steady family. The other is unemployment.

To keep my picture in balance I ought now to give from my three hundred story after story of families reduced to dejection of mind and weariness of body and loss of all estate by unemployment. I ought to do it, but I will not. For one thing, if I began I should hardly know where to stop. For another, more is known about unemployment and its effects than about any of the other factors with which I have been dealing, more than about all of them put together.

True, the torrent of fact and figure and description seems to swirl round and past the imagination of many of the well-provided and the safely employed. But that may be in part a result of its very volume. It does not bear thinking about.

Only this will I say; that unemployment appears as both cause and effect in very many of the stories. To say that the long-unemployed are, taken by and large, the fag end of the labour market, the residue of not-very-employables, would be to give a false cast, a crooked twist, to the truth. The truth is that among the long-unemployed are many of low employability; but that as often as not it is unemployment that has helped to make them so. The longer you are out the worse you feel and the worse you look, and the harder it is to get an employer to say: "All right. I'll give you a start." What, instead, you hear is: "How long did you say you'd been out? Two years! Hm—well, I'll send for you if I want you."

What are you going to do about the man who falls into unemployment and sinks into unemployability, not through any initial demerit of his own, but by freak of adverse fortune; the closing of a pit, the shutting down of a mill, the coming-in of a labour-saving machine, the contraction of the market for the goods in which his skill lies? At best, treat him like one who is entitled to compensation for a wrong suffered. That is what Benefit is for. At worst, keep him and his family alive. That is what the Means Test is for. Train him or condition him for other work and try to get him moved to where things are not so bad. That is what the Training and Transfer Schemes have done. Help him to overcome the obstacles that stand between him, in his pennilessness, and the chance of a job: spectacles, dentures, rig-out, and so on. That is the task the Unemployment Assistance Board should undertake, and has done so nobly in some areas. All that. But is it enough?

I will not set about an answer to that question. It is not my present business, which concerns the effect of these things on the distribution of the nation's privately ownable wealth. I will only say that so long as we have unemployment on any large scale, and particularly if we have a Means Test, we cannot very well expect anything other than that four million of our twelve million families should count their possessions at nothing or less than nothing; for unemployment runs neck and neck with sickness as a cause of our having such a mighty propertyless multitude among us.

Two other causes I will mention of households being in shadow instead of in substance. One is

failure in business. I could recount to you a dozen
or more such cases merely from my three hundred
sample. The big store and the multiple shop, in
their onward march, tread with heavy feet (I could
almost say stamp with heavy feet) on the little
shopkeeper. The business on which he or she had
depended for a livelihood declines or is crushed and
dies, the shutters go up, and the owner of the
business (man or woman) sets out, often loaded with
debt, to find paid employ. Among the four million
of our twelve million families who have nothing or
next to nothing in hand, you will find more than a
sprinkling of these.

You will also find those who saved or came in
for a sum of money—an endowment policy, a compensation award, a commuted pension, or what-not
—and who sank their all in a business venture. Be
chary of advising working folk who have a little
sum in hand to start up in business. It always looks
so promising at the start; it so often comes to grief
and throws the family into almost hopeless disorder
and penury and despair. Should I exaggerate if I
said that three out of four such ventures end in
disaster? The little shop, the wayside café, the
trading round, is not in these days (if it ever was) for
the inexperienced and the damaged. There are still
profits to be made in such ventures; but only by
those who have grit and gumption out of the
ordinary and who look and learn before they leap.

You will find, too, among the number, those who
lost their all to one of the catch-penny cheats who

specialize in defrauding humble families of their
nest-eggs. One of the mysteries of our national life
is our tenderness to the despoiler of the working-
class family and our rooted determination to wink
the other eye at his doings. I shall suggest the
reason to be that it is so difficult to see how his
little doings differ from some of the doings of big
business, and if you are going to pull him up for
what *he* does, where are you going to draw the line?
For one reason or another we allow him to carry
out his frauds with an immunity and an impunity
unequalled, so far as I can discover, in any other
self-respecting country on the face of our globe. I
shall have more to say on this.

One of the things I particularly wanted to know
about these poor and troubled families was the
extent to which they were in debt. The matter of
debt is one on which, as I have said, there has been
simply no available information whatever. So this
that I am about to relate concerning the three
hundred families is a glimpse into the previously
unknown.

Between half and two-thirds of these families were
in debt for smaller or larger amounts. The most
usual, or if you prefer it the typical, amount of any
one family's indebtedness was £5. That may not
seem very much; but I assure you that £5 is a colossal
sum. One-seventh of the families owed £20 or more.
That is a monstrous sum, from which there is no
foreseeable release apart from a win in the Pools.
I keep mentioning the Pools. The reason will appear.

Debts to whom? Debts for what? First and foremost, of course, for rent; and after rent, for rates. Two out of every five families were behind with the rent, some for a pound or two, but many for £5 and over. Then debts to pawnbrokers; but these are perhaps in a different category, for the pledges can be let go. Then debts to tradespeople such as grocers and milkmen. One family in ten had such debts, the most usual amount being twenty-five or thirty shillings. Next Hire Purchase obligations. One family in twelve were paying for goods got by signing on the dotted line; the sums ranging from a few shillings to as much as £15. Then debts to money-lenders, admitted by one in twenty of the families. A good deal of obscurity here. Then doctors' bills owing. The sums range from 10s. to £34. Many of them are of £5 and over. Finally debts to tallymen: and a few small borrowings from kindly friends.

Debts right and left among these poorest of poor families. To ask why they haven't possessions would be to prattle. What we have got to ask about them is, can they ever possibly get straight? To be straight would be next door to paradise.

This question of debts seemed to me at the outset a crucial one. In some lands debt is said to be the key to all labouring life. The money-lender is master; the labourer, months behind in his life reckoning, is his bondman. I wondered if anything of that kind obtained with us. Before we go too far into the question of how the pluses of our wealth

G

are parcelled out, we ought to know something of
the minuses.

In particular, I felt curious about four of our
small-loaning agencies; the money-lender, the pawnbroker, the hire-purchase dealer, and the loan club
in all its various guises.

The results of my explorings in these mysterious
regions must be stated in very few words. To do
them justice would require a book.

First, let me beg you not to think of any of these
systems of lending and borrowing as mere shifty
exploitation of the frailties of human nature. Even the
money-lender supplies what is in some part a
genuine need. So long as you have propertyless
families chronically or fitfully hard up, you will
have a need for the money-lender; and he or she
will arise to meet that need. The charges are high;
but the risk is great. Since the Moneylenders Act
the professional lender must be registered—or
ought to be. He or she may stipulate for any rate of
interest, but cannot recover in Court any portion
that is deemed "harsh and unconscionable."

My impression is that money-lending is on the
decline. The social service payments have at any rate
diminished the intensity and the frequency of
desperateness which used to drive families to the
money-lender. To-day, apart from the miserable
borrowings to which I have referred, resort to
money-lenders seems to go in patches. Why it should
be so I do not know. On some housing estates, I
learn, the money-lender is the bane of the neighbour-

hood. Other estates and working-class neighbour-hoods are almost free of him, so far as one can learn.

As I say, you must look on the money-lender as a boon as well as a bane. If you want to curb such of his activities as are evil you had better work with might and main to provide loan agencies for hard-pressed families in sore need, agencies that are not worked for private profit. Your churches and chapels, your clubs and societies, your Guilds of Help and Social Service Councils, your Co-ops and Trade Unions and Trades Councils, should be all contri-buting their quota to the provision of loan facilities for those suddenly in need of a financial advance.

Let me say a little more at this point upon the debit and credit cycle of life. It will come appro-priately here; for I am dealing with loan agencies and I am urging that more and better lending agencies are needed. Until such time as practically all families have enough inherited or accumulated wealth, enough of a private fortune, to tide them over the lean periods of a typical human life, you will need pools of wealth into which those who are in the flush period of life can pour their surpluses and from which those who are turning the tight corners of life can borrow.

I meet some who look with disdain on all borrow-ing. Their ideal seems to be a state of affairs in which everybody lends. They overlook, I think, the fact that unless you can find someone to borrow you will not be able to lend. Were there no borrowers, lenders would be in the soup. They would have to work for their living instead of living on their investments. So let lenders not look down their noses at borrowers.

You can, of course, lend for construction instead of for consumption. You can lend your money to be used as capital for production. In that way all of us could be lenders and drawers of interest on our lendings without the need for any borrower who has borrowed because he is in a tight corner.

But until that happy day, we shall, most of us, go through our days sometimes on the debit side of life and sometimes on the credit side.

I called this the debit and credit cycle of life. During some periods we are, all of us, in the debit phase; in other periods we are in the credit phase.

As infants and youngsters we live on the love and bounty of our parents. If we start work early and do well, we may repay a little of what we have had. We may (if we are old-fashioned enough) also save a little. But for the most part we come to maturity penniless.

If we now become engaged, we may start to save in earnest. There have been times when it would have been expected of us; but nowadays there is less need. We can furnish "the easy way." Even the wedding ring we can get on the instalment plan. The more fortunate of us borrow from the old folks. Most of us, I fancy, start married life in debt.

As the next three or four years go by, provided we are not ill or out of work, we pay off our loan and one day we are "clear." In the meantime we may have acquired a gas cooker, a sewing-machine, a radio, a cycle, and a little lawn-mower—all on the instalment plan; and the aggregate payments may come to a good many shillings a week.

If we can postpone the appearance of the first child long enough we can get "clear" with these also: we may even get a small sum in hand; though pints, pictures, perms, pools, smokes, and all manner of fripperies and elegancies will clamour for our coins. By resisting firmly we can, unless the income is at or below subsistence level, put something by.

If without undue delay the babies come, we may get behind once more. In spite of insurance services there are special bills, doctor's and chemist's—and grocer's too, perhaps, by and by—that may have to wait. The pram is on the dotted line, but a year or two clears that.

Some of us, of course, are improving our position and getting increments on our pay. If we advance rapidly enough and the old folks are not by this time needing aid we may keep level, and even get a little ahead; but the probabilities are that until our children have done their schooling and are out earning on their own account, we shall lag behind. Particularly will this be a tight period for us if we go in for fancy schooling.

But now the youngsters are all in work or gone; and by now perhaps we are on as full earnings as we shall ever make. Now, if we can resist the temptations to spend, we can really put by against a rainy day. Three out of four of us will not bother or not succeed.

After all, there's the insurance pension at 65 or the old-age pension at 70. But the minority of us will now be increasing our weekly payments into an endowment policy or our deposits in the Post Office. Now we rise from the debit into the credit phase of the cycle of family life.

By the time we retire or are retired we have a few hundreds in hand. It is for "a rainy day." We have saved it at great sacrifice in order that we may draw on it and live on it now. Alas for human nature! We dread the thought of drawing a penny of it, and the odds are we die in pinched circumstances with the bulk of it still in cold storage. It is divided among our kith and kin, who quarrel more than is seemly over the trifle that comes to each.

We, however, who leave enough to be worth more than a passing glance by the tax-gatherer are few and far between. The vast majority end their lives, as they began, with nothing to speak of. Whichever it may be, the life cycle of debit and credit is complete.

I stress this point of the debit and credit cycle of life, in which the typical person is normally at some periods in funds and other periods in debt; for in so far as you think it impossible to ensure that every family shall have its nest-egg, or that every youth shall have a claim on the community for a lump sum on marriage, and every householder a claim to a lump sum on the birth of a child, just so far must you see either the need for a pooling system like the old mutuality clubs, whereby those in the debit phase can borrow at reasonable rates from those in the credit phase, or you must admit the reason and justification for the immense spread of credit buying. Indeed, I shall be asking you to consider the whole business of hire purchase and instalment buying from the standpoint of a pool from which those in the need can draw temporarily from those in funds.

What I have just said had to do not with poor families, but with all families not belonging to the monied class. But now back to our poorest families. The money-lender and the loan club I have dealt with. Now the pawnbroker.

Pawnbroking, too, is on the decline. In twenty-five years the number of pawnbrokers has decreased by 30 per cent. Again I think the social service payments have made it less necessary to have to resort to pawning. But hire purchase may also have contributed by filling houses with goods which may not be pawned until they are clear. Then again, it is a long way from the housing estate to carry the marble clock or the eiderdown. The majority of pawnbrokers' customers are still working-class people, but there is far less of the habit of weekly pledging. To meet this change pawnbrokers have in recent years been trying to increase their business by advertising to the middle-class public—offering them an alternative to the money-lender in times of financial embarrassment.

Pawnbroking is on the decline, but it is by no means dead. Here are a few figures. They are for one branch of a pawnbroking business in a working-

class district of London. In one month seven
thousand pledges were taken; £2,500 was lent on
them; five thousand pledges were redeemed; the
interest amounted to £100 and the ticket money to
£50. Pawnbroking declines, but it still plays a
large, and if I may say so, honourable and serviceable
part in working-class life. Do not look down your
nose at the pawnbroker unless you can point to a
better agency of your own creation where the
equivalent of his services can be obtained.

One-third of my three hundred families had goods
in pledge with the pawnbroker. With one family
in seven the dependence on the pawnshop was
systematic. There was weekly pawning.

In ever-greater proportion the goods pledged are
not redeemed. In these days of changing fashions
and cheap grades they lose value heavily in the
twelve months during which they must be in pledge
before selling. So in these days the pawnbroker's
lot is not a happy one.

The Money-lender, the Pawnbroker, and the Hire
Purchase Dealer: those were the first three of the
debt agencies I mentioned. Hire Purchase is of
course in different category from the others. It is
curiously enough the exact opposite of pawnbroking.
In the one you lodge goods and acquire a loan; in
the other goods are lodged with you and you acquire
a debt. But Hire Purchase concerns the thriving
more than the poverty-stricken. I will deal with it
in my next chapter.

But one more thing I must say about these

poorest families before I leave them. I must speak of their pitiful savings.

What, savings! These! Yes. Over half saved up something week by week—if only a few pence. For what? Why, how else would they ever get a pair of boots or any sort of a rig-out? One quarter of them saved systematically just for clothes. Then came the few pence for the Hospital Savings Association. A few pence for a sickness club. And then, almost universal this, the shilling or one and six or two shillings for Life Insurance, which means Burial Insurance.

Yes these, even these, the better half of them, save their few coppers, their weekly bit of silver. Not with any hope of accumulation; but that they may have a handful of coins with which to buy clothes; to buy a poor claim on admission to hospital should they fall ill; and to buy the means of mourning in the event of a death and security against that ultimate horror and degradation—a pauper's grave for themselves or for any member of the family.

Blessed are those among them who can shop at the Co-op. But if you are below a certain level of living you find you have to forgo the boon of the Co-op with its quarterly divi. You must buy where you can pick up left-over scraps or where you can get tick. Only one in ten of my three hundred families shopped at the Co-op. Those one-tenth had the inestimable advantage of being able to draw, once a quarter, a lump sum in the shape of divi. Call it if you like a veiled form of compulsory saving.

I will allow you that, and still call it a priceless boon.
Indeed, I will say now, and I am going to say still
more emphatically by and by: if that is veiled compulsory saving let us have more of it, and more
and more. Let us have features introduced into our
social and political system which will result in large
numbers of families receiving lump-sum divis in
one guise or another.

Among the "savings" are the pence paid away
week by week for Burial Insurance. They pay,
these poor families, their sixpence and shilling and
two shillings a week to make sure, as they hope, of
decent mourning and a proper funeral. Some of
us are inclined to scoff. Why should we? Rather let
us rail at the system under which more than half
the pitiful sums they pay goes in expenses and
lapsed policies. Not sixpennyworth of value do
they get for any shilling so hardly spared. Is it not
time we did what all other self-respecting countries
have done—put burial insurance on the health card?
I will say more about that in what follows.

And they spend silly money on the Pools! Yes,
lots of them do. Well, wouldn't we? Apart from the
Co-op Divi and a sudden death it is the only chance—
I mean gambling of any sort, but particularly Football Pools—it is the only chance of a lump sum of
money ever coming their way. Of course they go in
for the Pools. The Pools have flourished and will
flourish whatever you say or do, because they are
catering for a hunger—the hunger for a lump sum—
to which we good people have given no concern.

We have got to learn from the Pools something of the natural needs of those who go in for the Pools.

But what about low wages as a cause of the poverty of these three hundred families? I cannot tell you from their records as I have them here. I should need to know their past earnings and history, and I don't.

For the part played by low wages in the causation of poverty you do better to look at the results of more general investigations. Take the survey of the standard of living in Bristol in the late 1930's, a better than average place in a better than average period. The enquiry showed that 10 per cent of Bristol's working and lower middle-class families could not afford to purchase even the very meagre amounts of food, clothes, fuel, light, and cleaning materials taken as minima for the purpose of the survey, without sacrificing other essential needs such as provision for sickness, savings, holidays, and re-creation. Another 20 per cent of the families, though not suffering the same poverty, stood precariously on the border line. One-fifth of the children covered by the survey were living in families below the poverty line and another third in families with seriously scanty means.

The upshot of my own analysis of the three hundred families, supplemented by the results of such enquiries as those at Bristol and elsewhere, lead me to the general conclusion that about one-tenth of our families do not receive enough to keep body and soul alive without shifts and stratagems.

Their children go underfed and badly clad. It is true that even they spare a little for diversion and that they skimp their already inadequate incomes by devoting trifles to the Pools in the hope of getting the windfall which is the only hope they see out of their wretchedness. One-third of our families, including that one-tenth, are little, if any, above the poverty line, for what they squander they can ill afford, what they save is saved at peril of their sustenance.

If you really want to see a populace which has some substantial share in the privately ownable wealth of our kingdom, these lower third of our families must (*a*) find ingenious ways of economizing and must save their economies, or (*b*) their incomes must be raised until there is a margin for saving, or (*c*) some system must be instituted whereby small parcels of that £20,000 million of privately ownable wealth can be transferred from its present ownership to the ownership of poorer families.

But remember that I am not dealing with privation and want. I am dealing only with why people haven't a little money in hand. I have looked into the lot of the very poor. I have shown they include the shiftless, the thriftless, the people with kinks and records, those who went under from sickness and unemployment, those who failed in business, those who fell among thieves, and those who are in tight corners. They include poor sorts and good sorts. Remember, all these as forming the lowest sediment of our society. Rule them out from any question of laying by a store of worldly goods. Prevention, not cure, is the hope. Windfalls are a possible way out here and there. They are in your four million. But there is now to be looked at the great centre block of families who manage to do themselves pretty well, and ask how it comes about that *they* own so little of the massed wealth of the nation. That is for my next chapter.

CHAPTER IV

POP GOES THE WEASEL

Now for the middle eight million families who you would have thought really could have been steadily putting by if they had a mind to. There has been enough coming in to provide a margin, narrow or wide. But with one thing and another, they have next to nothing in hand from pay-day to pay-day; or at most a hundred or two pounds.

Middle eight million! Where have they suddenly appeared from? And how?

Why, I dealt in my last chapter with those who have no margin whatever to save on. I was dealing with the families who, so far from storing up riches can hardly eke out their pitiful incomes. Families out of sorts, out of fortune, out of favour—out of everything but wretchedness and debt.

I did not try to put a figure on them. But now I am venturing one. I will put them at two million. Families mind, not persons. That is more a figure of speech than a figure of fact: but I fancy it is not far out. The families whose income is not enough to provide basic needs have been put by other calculators at 15 per cent to 20 per cent. My two million would make 17 per cent. It cannot be far out.

So I've put on one side, as already dealt with, two million families at the bottom. Then at the top I am also putting a paling, for present purposes, round another two million families who range from quite nicely off to immensely rich. By quite nicely off I mean those with anything from a few hundred in the bank upwards. You will see I am keeping my definitions vague. But here at the upper end are the families who have a bit of money, and who come in for a bit of money. Also, of course, those with tons of money who come in for tons of money.

That is, two million at the poorer end and two million at the richer end. Stand those away and we have got left a middle eight million families who, though they fare not too badly in the matter of income and ought, one would think, to have a fairish sum in the locker, own in fact somewhere between nothing at all and a mere hundred or two pounds.

I will not ask why do they not save and bequeath and inherit; for some of them do. I will put it this way: why do not *more* save and bequeath and inherit *more*? Why do not *more* own *more* of the aggregate wealth of this rich and increasingly flourishing land? Why do they let the two million at the top have and hold the bulk of the privately ownable wealth of the nation, and content themselves, in their multitudes, with the leavings: the loaves in the cupboards of the few and the crumbs in the fingers of the many. There is the question. What is the answer?

Is not part of it again contained in that retort: "What do you expect? You know what people are"? He was talking not only of the poorest of the poor. He was talking no less of this multitude that could accumulate if it had a mind to (in that it has enough coming in) but does not.

Do we not know those who, making pounds and pounds a week, never have a penny to bless themselves with? They are the sort who have just no use for the future. The happy-go-lucky. Eat, drink, and be merry; and let to-morrow go hang. Or give here and give there, help this poor creature and help that —out of the goodness or the softness of the heart— and leave the day of want to the ravens.

And do we not know those for whom nothing will serve but to live a month or two, or a year or two, ahead of their income: who follow that well-known precept: "If you wait till you can afford it you'll never have it."

Do we not know them all? Even here, in not-too-bad, and in easy circumstances? Even here, among the earners of fair-to-middling incomes? The thriftless; the shiftless; the fritterers; the ones with the holes in their pocket? Don't we know them? We ought to. Many of us see one each morning in the mirror.

And do we not know the sort that seems to go through life looking for someone who will relieve him of his fortune? The predestined mug, the gull, the flat, the noodle. They are mostly the ones who lust after something for nothing and cannot or will not see that what they are heading for is nothing for everything. Snapping at the shadow they part with the substance. Who shall raze out from the tricky little Smart-Alec corner of the mind the craving to be bamboozled?

But, of course, here too are the victims of sheer ill luck; even here, among the not-too-badly incomed. Here, too, is the one who had a long spell of sickness which took the last penny of the thousand pounds that had been saved through so many years.

Here is the chief clerk who was without a job for eighteen months during which not only did everything go but debt was piled up. Does anyone who hasn't been through it know how the money goes when the rent and the rates have to be paid and food and clothing bought, and appearances kept up—with nothing coming in? He's in a job again now. Earns his six pound a week (instead of six hundred a year). But he counts now among the debtors rather than the creditors.

Here, too, just as among the poorest, is the shopkeeper whose business was trodden on by conquering multiple or department or Co-op store or left high and dry by the new motor 'bus service, or devastated by the closing of a works or a pit, or dragged down by bad debts allowed by over-much pity, but who kept enough from the ruin to stay above poverty level and to help him into the ranks of the earners.

Here too is the one who was not a Smart-Alec mug craving bamboozlement; who was a decent, honest, trusting venturer; and who was robbed of all he had by clever scoundrels operating always just on the safe side of the ramshackle law. It isn't so much what he has lost that puts him and leaves him where he is, among the wealthless; it is the sense of having been "done" and the knowledge that he lives in a land where such things are winked at—perhaps because if they were not some other things in which quite highly placed persons are engaged might also have to be looked at without winking.

Here too, of course, is the persistent punter; the frequenter of the dog tracks; the plunger in the pools; the twiddler of the fruit machine; the fiddler with the pin-table, and the devotee of "Horsey, Horsey." Does he belong with the mugs; or is he a class to himself?

I think he is in a class to himself. First cousin to the mug. He is not taken in, he walks in. He gets, or he thinks he gets, in hope and thrill fair value for what he loses; but his judgment is somewhat addled. And when I say he I mean equally she.

We shall have to look more closely at these and other classes. But first, how far is it true, even of this middle eight million families, let alone the bottom two million, that they do not get enough to save on? Or, if you like, that they do not get a square deal in the matter of wages or incomes?

There is the disquieting fact I quoted in my first chapter: that eleven and a half million of our income receivers got less than £2 10s. a week; that their average was £2 a week; and that while they form two-thirds of all income recipients they receive only one-third the total income.

Then how far is it just under-payment that puts

a good many of these, even the middle eight million who have enough to live on, in the ranks of the propertyless—and keeps them there? I don't know. I can put no measure on it. No doubt even among these, while many have enough for rent and food and clothing by any accepted standard of efficiency, they have not much beyond that to spare. But if they had more, would they save more?

They might; but if experience counts for anything it would be but a fraction of the increased income.

No reason there, of course, for withholding more generous pay. That is not what I am saying. What I am saying is that except on the poverty line and below poverty line, lack of saving and lack of possessions is not an effect of lowness of income; and greater saving with a greater spread of private wealth would not necessarily follow from a raising of the income level. Other beneficial things would follow, but not that. Not with any certainty.

For as the income rises we become little by little more lavish in our ways and in our ideas of what our ways ought to be. Between 1924, shall we say, and 1938 there was an increase of 12 per cent in the real wages of workpeople generally. By that I mean that because of the lower food and other prices in 1938 as against 1924, the rather higher wages buy 12 per cent more of those things on which the housewife spends the wages than could be bought with the wages in 1924. There is a margin for saving! Wage-earners and smallish salary-earners as a body need only have kept to 1934 standards of living and banked the rest to have had laid away by now . . . but wait a moment, that shall come later.

If only they had saved instead of spent the addition to their incomes—as a class I mean. If only! But they didn't, of course. Keeping the extra in hand may be all right for a month or two; but who wants it to go on for fourteen years?

No, it has been spent. On what? Well, a good deal of it has gone, of course, in better feeding and clothing and housing and furnishing and reading and holidaying—and quite right too. But it has also gone, along with what was already going in such directions, on pools, perms, and pints; on cigarettes, cinemas, and singles-and-splashes; on turnstiles, totalisators, and twiddlems: and on all manner of two pennyworths of this and of that. To how much of that shall we say "and quite right too"? Let not a hardened sinner like myself give the answer.

We had better have the figures. Let us start with the Demon Drink? He has, of course, a long history. Though statistics are lacking, we can be sure that he was on the scene centuries before Noah, and was making Britons merry or mad ages before Alfred burnt the cakes. When James the Second lost his throne to the tune of "Lillibullero" our fathers were drinking two barrels of hefty beer per head per annum compared with half a barrel of more watery beer to-day. Since the day I first opened my eyes upon a drink-sodden world, beer consumption per head had by the 1930's fallen one-half; spirits per head had fallen to one-fifth; and wine per head had fallen by a little.

We drink less but we pay more. In those earlier years of the eighteen-eighties we paid £4 a head for our strong drink of one sort or another; in 1938; we were paying for the far smaller indulgence £5 per head. Much of it, of course, goes in taxation. In 1880 the duty on beer was 6s. per standard barrel of potent liquor; in 1938 it was 24s. per barrel for what the Elizabethans would have called "small ale," £250,000,000 a year being spent on our fermented beverages, which is three times as much as we spent on boots and shoes, or on motor cars and cycles, or on coal. The toll taken by the tax-gatherer in 1938 was nearly half the purchase price.

So we are a soberer people than we were a century or half a century ago; but we spend more on our lesser and milder potations and the Chancellor of the Exchequer takes a very large part of what we spend and cuts a dash with it in all directions.

But it might, of course, still be true, not so true as once but still true, that the wealthlessness of the multitude is largely a matter of drink. Mr. Rowntree ascertained that 11 per cent of the poverty he found in York was due to drink. That means, of course, that 89 per cent of the poverty was due to other causes, and anyhow it is always a matter of opinion how far the drinking causes the poverty and the poverty the drinking. The Liverpool Social Survey led to the view that not one in twenty of the poorest had visited the public-house, so far as could be ascertained, during the week of the enquiry. My own information as to the causation of poverty in the very poorest families gives a picture in which drink hardly appears.

What shall we say, then, to drink as a cause of the wealthlessness of our populace? These three things, I suggest. First, there is no evidence that the richer drink less per head (or less per headache) than the poorer; second, that if the desire or need for fermented liquor be regarded as excusable or right, then the imposing of smashing drink taxes is inexcusable in that it drags revenue from the drink-needing poorer out of all proportion to their incomes; and third that even on the darkest showing drink plays but a small part in the wealthlessness of our millions. According as you feel about it, drink is a Racial Poison or an excursion ticket to Paradise, Hangover, and all stations beyond. Give Drink its place; but don't exaggerate it. We have many newer, more convenient, and fussier means of getting fuddled.

For instance, there is that queer liking we have developed for getting our laryngeal passages all a-soak and our nervous systems all a-twitter with something called nicotine. We do it by continually burning under our noses leaves and twigs wrapped in paper or stuffed into retorts and gasping in "as deep as to the lungs" the reek of the burning. Anything that will give our hands something to fiddle with, and especially anything with a bit of flame and fug to it, and even more especially something that will take us out of ourselves, is a boon for which we would willingly go without food or turn out to a slot-machine in a pea-soup fog.

Eight out of every ten men are given over to this curious practice, and four out of every ten women. In the course of it we conflagrate under our noses 80,000 tons of fermented leaf-mould a year. We spend on it £160,000,000; for it is costly stuff. Again the tax-gatherer takes the larger share of what we spend; and hands over to the Exchequer £83,000,000 a year.[1]

There is no distinction to be observed, so far as I know, between rich and poor in their devotion to this procedure of stupefaction by smoulder; but again the better-off need spend on it no more than pin-money, whereas the poorer can, and some do, part with up to a tenth and more of their incomes to get the same degree of dazedness. A great part of the increase in late years has been due to the spread of this strange proceeding among women, who previously merely sat by and coughed.

There is no particular moral to be drawn from this extension of the tobacco habit, except that a people left to its own devices and to the wiles of advertisers will find curious ways of getting rid of any additional surplus income; and that anyone who wants to see the unpropertied citizenry of our

[1] The sum spent on tobacco has more than doubled since these words were written, and by far the larger part goes into the Exchequer. The figures quoted relate to pre-war tobacco consumption and cost.

land become larger participators in the private
ownership of the nation's wealth is going to have
his work cut out and had better put his thinking cap
on. For one thing he will have to produce a breed
which can be happy in its environment with but
mild doses of lightly taxed drugs or none at all.
Then he will have either to distribute lumps of
ownership raised by some automatic contrivance, or
set up a savings campaign outrivalling in effective-
ness the selling campaigns of the drug sellers.

While still on drugs let us take the cinema. In recent years we have spent £40,000,000 a year or more
in going to the pictures; and of that the ever-zealous
tax-gatherer took his share to the tune of £7,000,000
a year. There were only 46,000,000 of us all told,
including infants in arms and centenarians; but we
took 20,000,000 tickets at our picture palace
pigeon-holes a week. (Some of us, of course, go two,
three, and four times. It is estimated that 40 per cent
of the population goes once a week, and of these
about two-thirds, or say 25 per cent of the total
population, go twice or more.)

We can no longer live, naturally, without the
Pictures. How could we? We rubbed along pretty
well without them not so long ago; but that was
because we played the fiddle, and whistled with a
warble, and read aloud passages grave or gay from
our favourite author, and even gave recitations. We
cannot do that any more, or we do not like to—in
these days when anyone can see Gracie or Shirley
for a few pence. So now we pay our pence or

shillings and sit in the dark and gape at and gulp
down what is fed out to us on fathoms of celluloid
tape.

£40,000,000 a year! But who, I would like to
know, is going to begrudge the propertyless man
or his wife or his son or daughter or his sister or his
cousin or his aunt their seat at the pictures? Not I,
certainly. All I want to do is to point out the obvious;
that what you spend you do not save, and what
you do not save you cannot hold or pass on. That
is all.

And it is no real pleasure to be at the pictures,
either, at any rate for a lady, and especially a young
lady, unless she has got the latest perm and has
done her face with the proper night lotion and day
lotion, and has had her eyebrows put in a more fetch-
ing place, and has got her lips done into a ruddy
blob and her fingernails varnished the colour of stale
blood, so that you expect the flies to settle on them.
Our women-folk have spent in the 1930's £1,500,000
a week, a *week*, mind you, on beautifying themselves
from the neck up and the wrist down. According
to advertisements in the papers there are others
who go in for a schoolgirl complexion all over, but
as to that I can offer no first-hand testimony. I am
told that in British factories alone 1,300 tons of face
powder and rouge, and 1,600 tons of face cream
were manufactured annually during these years. I
am told that the lipstick manufactured in the same
period in Great Britain would reach, laid end on end,
from Leicester Square to Fairyland and back. So

£80,000,000 a year can go in painting the lily and perming the daisy. And why not, pray? Who is going to begrudge miss or madam her charcoal eyebrow? Not I, certainly. What is sauce for the Mayfair gander is sauce for the Middletown chick. All I say is that what you spend you cannot save, and what you do not save you cannot have and hold. If with the rising standard of incomes there is a greater margin, it has to escape many hazards before it reaches the money-box.

And then we like to have our little bit on. A shilling or two, or a half-crown or two. With the street bookie, or the barber, or the fellow at the works. Or an evening at the dogs, once a week say, in the season. Or we exercise what it pleases us to call our minds in composing Bullets and backing our fancy to the tune of some multiple of sixpence; or we give the better part of our Sunday to pondering the order of popularity of twenty Radio stars or twelve smart bathing costumes (or rather we seek to guess what others like ourselves will guess that others like themselves will guess to be the order of popularity), and we back our judgment with good money and hope for a prize. And millions and millions of us, who never speculated before because it wasn't quite the thing, have given Thursday night to the filling up of our football coupons and have sent our shilling or five shillings a week to the pools. Formerly speculative investment of this sort was the prerogative of the flash, the frolicsome, the footling, the fishy, and the feeble-minded—who have always backed horses, bought sweep tickets *sub rosa*, and played pitch-and-toss in the alley or *chemin de fer* in the parlour. But recently it became the regular preoccupation of one in three. This is one of the most momentous happenings of our time. We'd better have some figures.

The all-over expenditure on that part of speculative investment called "betting" or "gambling" is thought to be round about £500,000,000 a year.[1] I say "that part of" because the sum just mentioned does not include the immense sums devoted to playing pitch-and-toss with trade or industry on the Stock Exchange, and elsewhere. Nor does it include the gigantic volume of wagering transactions in which members of the public lay with insurance companies weekly bets on the odds of their dying, or annual bets on the odds of their smashing up their cars or having a fire or being burgled. The £500,000,000 is for betting other than through stock-brokers or insurance agents.

Now you will not need to be told that the £500,000,000 is a turnover and not an expenditure. When two bet together, what one loses the other gains. When ten bet with a professional book-maker or a pool promoter, a part of what the six lose the four gain. Only a part. For the bookie must live. And the pool promoter must live. The professional men must not only live but must pay their toughs and touts and tic-tacs and indoor staffs and printing and postage bills and newspaper adver-

[1] A pre-war figure, of course.

tisement charges. So although the £500,000,000 goes, like sweet music, round and round and round, it goes in a leaky pail. How much of the £500,000,000 leaks away in a year's round and round? Again, no one knows. I should say it cannot be less than £100,000,000. I mean net leakage from the pockets of the public, either right down the sink —sheer waste—or into the pockets of the professionals—out of which, of course, they must pay their expenses. I am sure it is not less than £100,000,000. It may be as much as £200,000,000.

Now so far as I am aware there has been no great increase in the numbers of the public who like to back their opinion as to which of several horses known to them only by name can and will run faster than the rest; nor in the total of their backings. There may have been a decline. But if interest in the performance of the horse has waned, there has waxed exceedingly interest in the performance of dogs running after an imitation rabbit and of players skilled in the art of kicking an inflated leathern sphere across a field against organized resistance.

During the twelfth year of dog racing, the sport was paying over £400,000 in prize money. Its controlling body had on the registers 60,000 greyhounds and 30,000 owners. Greyhound "fans", according to a Sunday paper, numbered 30,000,000; which, if it were true, would mean two out of every three of us—men, women, children, and tender babies in loving arms. I don't think it can be true;

but without question the number is large. Between two seasons £500,000 was spent in erecting new totalisator machinery in what are called the Super-Stadiums. In one of these, one Derby Night, £100,000 went through the machines in four hours. At another, the operators can deal with 27,000 bets a minute. A minute, mind you! And still there are people who pretend to have doubts about human progress.

Even so, the onward march of the Dogs was nothing to the outward spread of the Pools.

It was Parliament that invented, thinking it was doing the opposite, the principle which has been the making of the Pools. Surely never in history has a Parliament made such a back-handed stroke. It ordained that there must be no cash betting on the Pool system. The promoters thereupon pulled their faces and resigned themselves to receiving entries one week and receiving the money for them the next week. It seemed so cumbersome. But behold, it was the veritable magic of all magics for getting and keeping a grip on the public. First week free, as it were, nothing to pay; then week after week to the end of the season not a chance, not a fear, of dropping out! You *must* send your money or be blackballed on all the lists of all the Pools; and while you're sending last week's money it would be simply absurd not to send a coupon for next week. As Educated Evans was wont to remark in his circulars "What a Beauty! What a Beauty! What a Beauty!" And a British Parliament invented it. Never forget that, when people say that nothing brilliant can come from an elected assembly.

Naturally, then, the Pools flooded the land in a few years. In 1930 they hardly existed. A few years later, every other adult in the land filled up a weekly coupon. Ten million people sent to the Pools, week by week, their sixpenny or shilling or half-crown or more postal orders. To cope with the Pool-mail the Post Office had special postmen. In the towns where the Pool businesses were, it even had special depots. It issued postal orders by the million every week to Pool clients. The Pool promoters occupied vast premises and employed thousands of workers. They were probably posting to regular and prospective clients every week fifteen million letters, each with its highly tempting coupon with pictures and slogans and stories of great wins, and places for the current week's forecasts.

How much of the millions received by the Pool businesses was paid out is not very clear; but the principal firms are members of a body called the Football Pool Promoters' Association, which claims to restrict to definite and reasonable proportions the amount of the rake-off. There have been Pools that have failed, but the best-managed of those that survived are gold-mines. Indeed, gold-mines cannot be mentioned in the same breath. Gushing oil-wells rather. Provided you have bored the right hole, the money pours up of itself: so that if you are not quick with the barrels it will drown you.

The newspapers are deep in it. They have drawn as

near as can be reckoned £20,000 a week in the season from Pool advertisements. The Post Office does pretty well out of it too. The poundage on postal orders bought has amounted to £3,000,000 a year.

So far as can be judged, the Pools have not only come to stay but come to spread. It is so easy and pleasant to slip in; such a bore to get out. No Parliament in any foreseeable future is going to have the nerve to give a nasty look at a business which has postal access for forty weeks in the year to two-thirds of our homes. Suppose the Pool promoters, in the course of their chatty week-by-week message to their clients, were to pass remarks about the Government! Who could measure the effect on votes? And, for that matter, what Parliament would care to interfere with the chosen recreation of ten million people? No! Parliament hath given, but Parliament can never take away.

Even allowing for the magic of the back-handed invention, does not the growth of the Pools point to the meeting of some real need? I do not mean now the thrill of pitting your wits against others and your luck against fortune. I do not mean mere distraction from hours of yawning boredom. I examined all that in a little book I issued a year or two ago entitled: *Why I Go In for the Pools* (London: George Allen & Unwin, Ltd., 1s.).

I mean rather that it may be in accordance with some need of our nature that there should be prizes flying about and descending without rhyme or reason on Tom and Dick and Harry, and on Peggy and Joan and Kate, who happen to have "come up" on a Pool. After all, is there not a great deal of chance in life generally and in fortunes as we find them? May not the craving for irrational windfalls be a rational craving? Ought we not to take stock of the fact that the vast majority of us, apparently, think it an excellent scheme that we should each and all pay a proportion of our incomes weekly in order that some, by an ounce of good management, allied to a ton of good luck, should get a fortune? Apparently we don't ask for any assurance that it should be ourselves. So long as someone is sure to get it and we have the remotest chance of being that someone it is all right.

Such of our leisure moments as we can spare from the pin-table, the pictures, the beauty parlour, the stadium, the fun fair, and the coupon—we appear to devote to signing on the dotted line. We hold with Edgar Wallace that "If I wait till I can afford it I shall never have it."

There is a good deal to be said for that view. Vast numbers of people to-day possess substantial and useful articles—bicycles, pianos, radio sets, and what-not—which they would never have possessed had it not been for hire purchase.

This practice of getting things at once and paying for them by instalments goes back a long way. Its beginnings are lost in obscurity; but as a trading system it was going strong a hundred and fifty years ago. Some of the oldest trade societies in our country are the Credit Traders' Organizations. In the past decade four of them have celebrated their centenaries.

The Credit Trader was (and is) the man who would let you have the stuff, indeed, persuade you to have the stuff, right away, though you hadn't a penny in hand, and would come round every so often to collect the instalments. He was the man who in due course, when your debt was getting nicely down, would permit or persuade you to have something else, again to be paid for by and by. In some parts he was known as The Scotch Draper, in some parts as The Tallyman. The name "tallyman" reveals how old the system is. It goes back to the days when few customers could read or write, when particulars of the debt and its repayment were recorded in notches on a cleft stick—the two halves of which must tally.

It was not just clothing and fancy goods the tallyman handled. He was ingenious and adaptable. Right back in my childhood I was told of the tallyman who arranged for you to have false teeth on the instalment plan. This particular tallyman took one of his customers into court. He charged her with evading payment by assault and battery. "She not only tried to slam the door in my face," he said, "but she bit me. Bit me with my own teeth!"

You perceive there the transition from Credit Trading proper to Hire Purchase. If they were in truth still his own teeth, then it was not a deferred payment transaction but an early case of hire purchase.

But between deferred payment and hire purchase there sprang up the check-trading system. You had better know of it, for it is still very much with us. It is this. Clever fellows who see their gain in coming as middlemen between shop and customer print checks or vouchers, rather like bank cheques. Their canvassers go round to the houses and let housewives have these checks on a signed promise that they will pay for them, by instalments, the face value and a bit more. The check is ready money. The housewife goes off with it to the shop. It must be, of course, a shop that has undertaken to accept the checks. The housewife buys this and that, and the total is entered on the back of the check.

When the amount of the check is exhausted it goes back to the clever fellows who issued it. They pay the shopkeeper, but in paying him they deduct a commission of 10 or 15 per cent for having introduced the customer and stood all the risk. Meantime they proceed to collect, as I say, by instalments rather more than the face value of the check from the customer. Thus the customer has the goods and the trader has the trade and the money, and the check-printing money-lender has his scrap of paper and everyone's happy—except perhaps the shop-keeper at parting with a lot of his profit, and the customer at paying more for the goods than the cash price and at being saddled with a debt. For, of course, the customer is now in debt to the kind and obliging check gentlemen, who send round to collect the weekly instalment and are apt to turn nasty if the instalments are not forthcoming.

That is the "club check" or "mutuality check" system. Thousands and thousands of our families, especially in London, get their clothes and their boots and their drapery and their fal-lals by it. They are spending ahead of income, maybe paying through the nose (though that is not always the case): and of course they are for ever in debt. What begins as a present help in time of need becomes a habit that cannot be broken and a servitude that cannot be shaken off.

At the same time there was coming in, by quite another door, Hire Purchase. Even that is a century old. Half a century ago not only were household goods like furniture, pianos, and sewing-machines being sold on the hire purchase system, but also commercial goods such as machinery, wagons, and cabs.

By the turn of the century the house-to-house canvasser was well on the job getting signatures on the dotted line. But then came the thing that was the real making of Hire Purchase; the mass-production of repetition articles for popular use. The numbers who hankered after these, or who were induced by advertisement to hanker, were legion.

As the business grew, the shopkeepers could not carry the outstanding debts. So finance houses sprang up to lend money to the trader. Along with that, manufacturers of proprietary goods built up hire purchase financing funds. Bicycles, motors, gramophones, radios were increasingly sold on a hire purchase basis. Everyone was doing it now.

But all this did not knock out the Scotch Draper. He went on as before. The business of supplying more perishable goods, clothing, and household gear by the old method of warehouse and tallyman developed. Large businesses grew up, supplying their customers from warehouses and show-rooms through the medium of canvassers and collector-salesmen.

Services were also included in the operation of instalment enterprise; correspondence courses, curative treatments, surgical appliances, systems for producing those deadly military chests and knobbly muscles, and (as I have said) dental services, could all be had by signing on the dotted line.

It was not all easy money. Many agents and trusts no doubt did well by using the dotted line as a strangle-hold. But many were bitten with their own teeth.

The Co-ops have had to go into it. By insisting on cash they were losing good trade. They call their credit schemes "mutuality clubs." They are really only another version of the check and credit organizations; but there is a difference. You must be a member. You have therefore already a stake in the Society. They know you. Your credit is good. If anything goes wrong, they will not browbeat and bludgeon you. I do not know if Co-op mutuality pays. I doubt if it does. But it is probably good business, all the same. It is pooling, with most of its benefits and least of its evils.

What does it all amount to, this Deferred Payment trading in our national life? You will not be surprised, by now, when I tell you that no one has its measure. I have been coming to the view since I began these investigations that as regards social conditions and business practice affecting the common people of this land of ours, no one knows anything about anything that really matters.

What I give now is largely guesswork; but it is guesswork based on the best information and opinion I have been able to obtain.

The volume of Hire Purchase dealing probably increased by twenty times between 1918 and 1938. The proportion of goods sold on hire purchase terms in 1938 was as nearly as I can tell, furniture 50 per cent; radio sets, 70 per cent; bicycles, 90 per cent; sewing-machines 85 per cent; motor-cars 40 per cent to 50 per cent; gramophones, 60 per cent. I will put those into one general statement. It is a guess; but an informed guess. Two-thirds of all mass-produced, repetition-manufactured goods sold to householders are sold "on the nod," to be paid for this year, next year, some time, never.

Then I wanted to know how much money was lent at an average time by Hire Purchase Finance Trusts to dealers in respect of Hire Purchase transactions. The best estimate I can give is £30,000,000. Also it seemed to me important that one should have an idea of the gross amount of the instalment credit carried by tradesmen themselves. It appears to be about £20,000,000.

So the position, if these guesses are not too far out, is this. At any given moment in a normal trading year the public owes on deferred payment agreements £50,000,000 to traders in respect of goods for which they have signed onthe dotted line; and £30,000,000 of that is "laid off," if I may so express it, by the traders on to Finance Houses.

Now there have been dreadful things done in the name of Hire Purchase. There have been rascally catch-penny firms—some of them revelling in flowery advertisements so high-minded and sweet-natured that when you read them you think the millennium must surely have come—rascally catch-penny firms selling shoddy stuff at high prices and brutally issuing first "frighteners" and in the last resort summonses on any pretext or snatching back goods on which a large part of the agreed sum has been paid.

The Hire Purchase Act has put a stop to a good deal of that; though not to all. Wherever you have a wealthless people under debt obligation to crafty individuals and business houses and finance corporations there will be openings for dirty work at the cross-roads: and in every mortal company, even among business houses and finance corporations, there is usually to be found, in holes and corners, a dirty character or two ready for dirty work. So we must be vigilant. If the Act should turn out to have holes in it we must patch them. But let us not condemn all instalment selling because of the malpractice of a very few in what is for the most part a reputable and well-conducted trade.

And let us not go looking down our noses at all credit buying. Think! All the world's work is done on credit. If you work for weekly wages your employer has your services on credit till the week-end. In some professions the payment for services rendered is "deferred" till quarter-end (and very awkward it can be sometimes!) Nearly all commercial buying is done on credit. A vast deal of industrial production is done on credit. Credit is quite orthodox and quite respectable.

So let us not despise Credit Buying. Let us look on it rather as an alternative to the frittering away of income on trifles of the moment. Then we shall see it as a form of saving. After all, when you sign on the dotted line you *do* get your radio set or what-ever it may be. Buying durable articles that last long after the final payment *is* almost a form of saving. If you are to choose between a nation of fritterers and a nation of hire-purchasers I think you should plump for hire purchase.

But is that of necessity the alternative? Could we not have a nation that made it more of a rule to save before it spent and to make its purchases cash in hand?

Even as we give full credit to credit, let us not forget that credit for trade and industry is quite another matter from credit in the home. Credit in trade and industry means or ought to mean enter-prise and increased material well-being. Credit in the home means just debt in the home. True, there is an article of value there to show for it. But debt in the home is the devil in the home. It is best to keep the devil out. Let us have a people who can go with cash in hand to make purchases instead of signing on the dotted line.

It was as I pondered these problems that the queer thought came into my mind, to which I referred earlier in the chapter. Suppose the working classes— any definition you like—had rested content with the standard of living of 1924, and had saved all the improvement in real incomes which they have enjoyed from then until 1938. How much would the working classes have saved in that fifteen years?

I will give the best estimate I can make. They would have saved £3,000 million. Not by stinting or forgoing anything. But just by being content with life on its 1924 plane and putting aside the increment, on the principle of "What you've never had you'll never miss."

How about that? Now we have got a *real* £3,000 million; not a fake like the one I examined in an earlier chapter. An average of £300 per working-class family laid away in the bank. A well-spread average, too, and all in fifteen years, without any skimping or scraping whatever—how about that?

Yes, it sounds fine. But there are two terrible thoughts to be faced. Let us face them.

First, do we really *want* a nation of small capitalists? Don't we know what such people are? They put by for a rainy day; but will they ever bring out and use a penny of what they have put by? Don't we know only too well those who will not? Rainy day, indeed! Not if it rained, snowed, hailed, thundered, and lightened would they touch a penny. Do we really want that sort; hoarding and never spending?

And then have we not some cause to feel just a little uneasy at the prospect of millions of people with a bit of money in the bank? Is there anything more calculated to produce the worst type of petty bourgeois mentality and outlook than this business of having a bit put by? Is there any living creature more narrow-minded and more grasping and reactionary than the small capitalist?

These are what I will call the two minor horrors of saving. How much is there in them. It is true that many people will not, if they can help it, break into their nest-egg. But such an attitude of mind is not inevitable? Could not quite a different mentality be engendered? I think it could.

You can, if you so fancy, encourage saving for specific purposes. I have already mentioned Clothing Club saving. One of the oldest of our institutions is the Goose Club, designed to provide good fare at Christmas. Since holidays became a normal part of working-class life, there have sprung up Holiday Savings Clubs and Associations. There are saving schemes designed to provide funds for giving the children a start in their careers as they come of suitable age. These are specific or purposeful savings. There is room for a vast extension of such savings. This is one alternative to Deferred Payments and Hire Purchase: To save beforehand for your radio set or your beano rather than borrow and pay by instalments afterwards.

But are we going to limit our advocacy of working-class saving to those "specific" savings? Is anything beyond that reprehensible as leading to useless hoarding and a mugwump mentality. If we accept that point of view, what becomes of any aspirations we may have that the ownership of the wealth of our land should be more equally distributed?

Recall an earlier passage in this book. If the privately ownable wealth of Great Britain were evenly spread among its families, each family would enjoy an income of £1 a week interest on invested possessions over and above anything the family might earn. If we are going to say that specific saving is all right, but anything beyond that is hoarding and must be frowned upon, bang goes any possibility of the typical family having its earned income augmented by a slice of the country's unearned income.

Let us be for specific saving, but let us not for a moment accept the argument that working-class savings should there stop. Every human activity is open to abuse, and the accumulation of private property is one of those activities. The wise use of private means is a matter for education, training, experience, and propaganda. If we make up our minds that we want, as well as a widespread electorate, a widespread investorate, we must see to it that our property-owning multitude knows its job.

So the two minor horrors turn out not to be so

dreadful. But now for a much more frightening
monster. This is the major horror. Indeed, it is the
horror of horrors. What would happen to trade and
employment if the multitude started saving instead
of spending?

I have just told how much the working classes
would have saved in fifteen years if they had remained content with the real wages (the standard
of living) of 1924 and had put away in the savings
bank all the surplus after that year. It comes, as
I have said, to the staggering sum of nearly
£3,000 million.

But if the working classes had saved at the rate
of £3,000 million in fifteen years, what would
have happened to trade?

What is the answer? Well, first, how much actually
was saved over those years? I think I am not far out
if I assume that the wealthy few saved from 1924
to 1939 somewhere about £3,000 million. Suppose
the working classes had also saved £3,000 million,
what would the effect have been?

So frightening was this aspect of the matter that
I thought I had better take counsel of a colleague
much more knowledgeable than I in matters of
monetary theory and practice. I did so. I went to
Mr. R. F. Kahn. His opinion was that had the
working classes saved £3,000 million in those
fifteen years instead of spending it, the result
would have been a trade stagnation and depression amounting to disaster. The withholding of
that large sum from spending would have cur-

tailed and annihilated profits and so reduced capitalist saving, and would have diminished the taxable revenue of the country. There would have been more unemployed to support on a diminished revenue. There would have been a deficit, and the Exchequer would have had to borrow. The diminished saving of the capitalists, added to the increased borrowing of the Government, would have neutralized the £3,000 million savings of the poorer classes. The nation would have been no better off.

It would probably have been even worse than that. The very substantial decline in profits would probably have led to an actual decline in the output of capital goods, which leads to the paradoxical conclusion that as a result of the increased working-class saving the total saving of the community (and the total addition to its wealth) would have been actually reduced.

But Mr. Kahn holds this view conditionally. He holds it because in his opinion our monetary authorities would not have pursued a counter-balancing remedial policy. If you are going to have more saving by the working classes without any reduction of the saving on the part of the capitalist classes, then you must put a great deal more of your national energies into the creation of capital goods. Of course we could have swallowed without detriment £3,000 million of extra working-class saving in fifteen years, provided we had been appropriately more energetic in the building of revenue-yielding houses, factories, machines, plants, vehicles, and so on.

The point Mr. Kahn makes is that during the years from 1924 to 1938 we scarcely ever needed the whole of our available resources. A reduction in consumption would not, therefore, apart from such special action on the part of the monetary authorities (which he excludes as unlikely), lead to an increase in the output of capital goods. With our 1938 policies it would have become abortive because the labour released from the consumption goods industries as a result of working-class thrift would remain idle instead of becoming employed elsewhere.

So, you see, this major horror is really something more than a bogy, to be shown up and laughed at. There is, however, the saving condition to which I have called attention. It is that we could as a nation absorb and digest working-class saving on the scale I have indicated provided we had people in authority and in power who would adjust financial policy and practice to the new state of affairs.

An outburst of saving on the part of the working classes yielding totals equal to the investable savings of the capitalist classes would probably have had, and would have the result of reducing the value of all capital and of reducing by one-third or perhaps by one-half the interest yield obtainable on investments.

It is a good rule never to be scared by demonstrations of calamities that will happen if we all do the right thing. Do it and see. If the effect of widespread saving is to diminish the interest-value of all savings —very well. Instead of the typical family drawing a pound a week interest on its £1,500 it would have to be content with ten shillings a week. Everyone with invested capital would similarly have to be content with ten shillings in the pound. By way of compensation we should have a Brighter Britain with clusters of lovely little houses each in its own garden, each equipped and furnished as the ideal home should be, nestling in the valleys or fledging the hillside; or of stately mansions, fit for heroes to live in, replacing the warrens of our foul and foetid slums. And we should have, replacing our industrial slums, model factories, built for light and air and ease and health, equipped with every cunning machine and every labour-saving device. We should have schools that were a joy and an education to children and teachers alike, instead of vile hovels in which still much elementary education is carried on. Anyone who says that we are near the limit of wealth-yielding ways of investing additional capital in the improvement of Great Britain is, I think, talking foolishness and blind ignorance.

We should need, I agree, a new personnel in high places, with a new mentality. Well, we must have that anyway, or perish.

CHAPTER V

"THIS THING'S TO DO"

HAVE you noticed a trouble I have been having with my labels? Language is a clumsy and tricky instrument for expressing thoughts. In my title, and again and again in my text I have been driven to using words that really do not fit any intelligent thinking upon the matter in hand. I have freely used the words "rich" and "poor"; but even as I used them I knew that they muddled up things I particularly wanted kept distinct. You can be rich in possessions *and* in income. Or you can be rich only in income. Being rich in income, you can live like a lord, and yet have no possessions at all. Or you can be poor in both income and possessions. It is for this reason that I have been driven to using such words as "wealthless" and "propertyless." Ugly words—but what other can I use? "Penniless"? That won't do. You cannot call a man who lives beyond his £10,000 a year income "penniless." So little has this subject I am dealing with been inquired into that our language hasn't even words for it. "Rich" and "poor" are hotch-potch terms. What they try to designate they merely muddle. So whenever I have wanted to say exactly what I meant, I have had to use "wealthless" and "propertyless." If anyone can think of better terms, as to the meaning of which there can be no possible misunderstanding, I should be glad to have them.

My subject has not been poverty but wealthlessness. For present purposes I am concerned for poverty only in so far as it leads to wealthlessness—to having no part or lot in the ownership of the vast agglomeration of privately ownable wealth with which our country abounds. I hope I have made that plain.

But two in ten of our families are poor in both senses of the word. They have no possessions but pawntickets and debts; and their incomes are barely enough to keep body and soul together. Their children lack food, lack fortune, lack opportunity, lack joy. Another three out of ten families have only just enough coming in to make ends meet. Anything saved or squandered is mostly at the expense of things needful for proper living. Their children, too, are not going to have much chance in life. One here and there will rise; the ninety and nine will follow in father's footsteps. Doomed to take the mean jobs, draw the low wages, live the hand-to-mouth life.

Among these millions who are on the brink or down in the abyss are, of course, as I have told, the thriftless, the shiftless, the feckless, the twisted, the twisters, the wastrels, the wasters, the mugs, the gulls, the flats, and the ninnies.

They are to be found in every rank and station of life. It is only when he hasn't money and family behind him that he (or she) flops and flounders down into the ranks of the destitute. There is a tendency, of course, for him to drift that way. If some enemy mixes sand in your treacle there's a *tendency* for the sand to sink to the bottom: but it takes a long time, and a lot of it somehow seems to be so buoyed up by the richness and the viscosity of the surrounding treacle that it hardly sinks at all. Still, as I say, there is a downward trend. You will find more white-trash sand in the bottom layer of your social treacle-pot than you will in the upper layers. Even more, I fancy, than you will find in the topmost layer of all.

In the bottom-most layer of those who have no possessions and not enough to keep body and soul together, you will find quite a fair number who prefer giving to owning. If some fellow takes their coat, they give their cloak also. Asked to walk one mile, they walk twain. And you will find, too, those others, much akin, who set no store by worldly goods. They follow that strange young Man who wandered about Galilee saying such things as "Take no thought for the morrow," and "Lay not up for yourselves treasures on earth." They take all that as gospel, and act on it. So naturally they haven't a penny to call their own. And there they are, in that bottom layer who own nothing and live on next to nothing.

Then there are those who came a cropper, and those who fell among thieves. They are in the wealthless millions. They may one day work and skimp and save their way back into modest affluence —but they have had a nasty knock. They had substance; and they have lost it. Only too often, in losing it, they lose heart, lose faith, lose confidence, and lose hope.

Then there are those who never had any wealth but their own human worth—their decency, their industry, their integrity—never had substance, and so at the first dastardly onslaught from accident, sickness, or unemployment they went down into the ditch where every ruffian element that makes for poverty, seeing them helpless, sneaked to the spot to give them a sly kick and to tread them deeper into the mud.

I have said what to my mind it behoves us to do about these assassins, sickness and unemployment, who lurk in the shadows waiting to spring upon, to rob, and to maim decent folk who happen not to have been born in safe or in well-protected circles. So long as we allow any loss of estate or any degradation or even deprivation to be suffered by those who have the misfortune to be so attacked, so long are we failing in our elementary duties as members of a human community and an economic and political commonwealth.

But these are only two in ten of the population. Another six or seven are suspended between the heaven of relative affluence and the hell of gnawing want. They have a tiny amount of wealth, somewhere between £1 and £100. Finally, there is the select group above the salt, the denizens of the heaven of relative affluence, with their motor-cars and their radiograms, their theatre stalls and their night-clubs.

These are the people who have the lion's share of the nation's wealth.

It is time to take stock of our position. I have given you a large pile of facts, and a number of hypotheses to explain some of the facts. What are we going to do with them? Are we to leave things as they are, believing that all is for the best in the best of all possible worlds? Or are we to see if something cannot be done to alter a situation in which so many good and honest citizens find themselves at the bottom of the wood-pile along with the feckless and the shiftless, the deranged, and the warped rejects of our civilization?

First of all, then, let us settle the question of whether we are to let well alone or to change the distribution of wealth. To that, it seems to me, there can be no two answers. The present system of distribution stands condemned by any rational tribunal. It is haphazard. It is unjust. It is uneconomic. Moreover, it is unlikely to persist exactly as it is, even if we do pass by on the other side. The inexorable forces of history will change it anyhow, so we may as well exert ourselves to divert it into the right channels.

This is a Christian country. Most of the owners of the national wealth profess the Christian religion in one of its divers forms. They can, therefore, offer no reasonable objection to the principle of a fairer redistribution of the riches of this country. How it is to be done we will leave aside for the moment, but let nobody fear that I am about to propose a wholesale expropriation or to incite the mob to a pogrom of the rich. That is far from my intention. This is a civilized country, and we aim at doing what we must do in a civilized way. We have, remember, been steadily redistributing the wealth of the country by means of taxation for many years.

We take as our basis, therefore, the assumption that the capital resources, the wealth of this great nation of ours, needs to be more fairly and more economically distributed among its citizens—among the people of Great Britain. Let us start by examining what people need capital resources for. Then we shall be in a clearer position to determine how they can acquire and hold this additional wealth we are proposing to give them, or put them in a position to own.

What does the average citizen, who, you will remember, earns only a very few pounds a week, need more wealth, more capital resources for? This is a question I have already partially answered in earlier chapters, but it will be convenient to recapitulate here.

The most urgent need that most people have for capital is to enable them to minimize the onslaught of the unforeseeable calamities of sickness, unemployment, accident, and death of the bread-winner. I have already described the vicious snowball of worklessness and illness, how the onset of one makes the other almost inevitable if prolonged for more than a few weeks. Much is done already by the

community, in the shape of health and unemployment insurances, workmen's compensation, and
widows' and orphans' pensions. But not enough.
If it were enough there would not be the number of
piteous cases on record that there are. Until the
State, that is you and I, and everybody else, is
prepared to guarantee the citizen against his standard of living falling below a much higher minimum
than it can at present, there is a crying need for that
£300 per family to be brought from the bright
figments of politicians' fancies to the concreteness
of hard cash.

Then there are certain events which cannot be
classed as calamities, but which nevertheless are, in
sober fact, calamitous for countless families in
Great Britain to-day. I refer to the rearing and education of children and to the maintenance of aged
folk. In how many families to-day does the presence
of an extra child or a weary, worn-out old mother
or father spell penury and skimping and joylessness?
Until the State is prepared to guarantee an equal
opportunity to every child, in both nutrition and
education, and a tranquil close to the life of every
old person, until that happy day, I say, there is a
crying need for that little nest-egg to become a
reality.

Then there are other occasions queuing up for the
use of that small portion of the nation's capital that
on egalitarian principles would be every family's
rightful due. Remember, it cannot be more than
£1,500, and it has a lot of work to do. There are a

number of special occasions that occur only once in the average man's life that make heavy demands on capital resources. They are mainly connected with his launching out on the sea of life, his technical training for a trade or profession, his marriage, the furnishing of his first home, and the purchase of his first house. Some facilities do exist for raising the needful capital. There are scholarships, and some local authorities make loans to those undergoing technical training. Hire purchase is the loan agency of the home-maker, and the building societies do yeoman service for the home-buyer. There is, however, room for a number of special funds, with either State or voluntary capital, which would make loans for these special purposes to citizens with inadequate private capital resources. The marriage rate would surely leap up if such marriage loans were available on reasonable terms.

Capital is also needed for the purchase of a whole host of goods ranging from semi-necessities to pure luxuries, such things as radio sets, bicycles, and the furniture needed by an expanding family. This, however, is satisfactorily provided for by hire purchase arrangements, but there can be no doubt that it would pay everybody, if they had the money in hand, to pay cash down and make the repayments to themselves instead of to somebody who claims interest. To some extent clothing also comes in this category, but except for large items such as men's suits, clothing is a current expense and should not occasion any call on capital resources.

Finally, there are those people, right at the bottom of the pyramid, whose first use of any increase in wealth would be to pay off debts, to convert a negative sum of wealth into a positive one.

These, then, are the things for which capital is needed. How are we to get the capital to those who need it? It will not have escaped your notice that in the course of my summary of the needs I have frequently had to say: "If the State will not do so and so, then the individual needs capital." This leads us to a consideration of the two main ways of holding capital, individual ownership and collective ownership. Collectively owned capital may be further subdivided into ownership by the State or some smaller representative of the community, such as a borough council, or by a voluntary association or society. This book is about the private ownership of wealth, but we must not lose sight of the fact that much of the nation's wealth is already collectively owned, and that the solution to many of the problems I have raised may be found in an extension of collective ownership.

We see the municipalities with their housing schemes and with their water, gas, and electricity departments and their buses and so on. We see Government establishments increasing up and down the land, and we see (assuming ever greater prominence) Britain's latest invention in these spheres, the semi-public corporation such as the British Broadcasting Corporation, the Central Electricity Board, and the London Passenger Transport Board.

If it be true that while the amount of private property concentrated in a few hands has been increasing, the value of these publicly owned or publicly controlled enterprises has been increasing at an even greater rate, then perhaps things are going the right way and a solution of quite another sort is emerging. What are the facts?

So far as they are ascertainable they are to be read in Mr. Campion's book, to which I have already made reference, *Public and Private Property in Great Britain*. I will not give figures, I will only give you the impression that I myself get from studying them. It is that the growth in the value of publicly owned property relative to privately owned property in Great Britain is not nearly so great as one might have supposed. It would appear that on the most favourable interpretation the value of publicly owned property in our country is as yet not more than one-seventh the value of property privately held. Public property increases, but privately owned property increases nearly as fast.

Still, there is a slight trend towards an increase in the proportion as well as the volume of publicly owned capital wealth. It may not as yet have made any sensational showing, or have effected any radical change in the structure or the texture of our national economic life, but it has been going on, and it may be that we shall find a part of the solution of our problem along those lines.

The titles to property are almost as closely concentrated as ever, but the more we can contrive that block after block of property and enterprise comes under public ownership and control, the more widely dispersed will be the benefit of that part of the national wealth.

Let us be clear about the bearing of this on our problem. It would help to solve one part of it but not the other. The ownership of say £1,500 by the general run of working-class families would mean, let me recall, two quite distinct things. First a reserve from which to pay cash for everything bought, and to take advantage of good openings, and to fall back upon in time of emergency; and second, a source of income, say an extra £1 a week, over and above the family earnings.

Now the extension of the public ownership and control of property and of enterprise, provided the public enterprises were as efficiently and energetically run as any private enterprise, would certainly result in the equivalent of an addition to the income of the average member of the community; for either prices would be lowered, or benefits would be conferred, or taxation would be remitted, to the extent to which the profits made accrued to the public instead of to private persons.

But the extension of public ownership and control would, of course, provide nothing in the way of the private reserve fund in the family locker. If we want our typical family to have private means, we must take quite other and separate action.

Then come to the point. Do we really and truly want our typical British family to have private means?

Perhaps we don't. Perhaps we think it best that the ownership of capital should remain concentrated in the hands of a very few persons, who by long usage and family tradition have learned how to administer it most efficiently in their own, and incidentally in the national interests. Perhaps we think it best to let them have it and draw the proceeds from it while our Chancellor of the Exchequer taxes their unearned income more and more heavily for the benefit of the propertyless multitude, and our Government takes steps to see that any misuse of the capital vested in them is visited with heavy punishment in the shape of partial confiscation.

If that is our plan and our policy, then we shall be perhaps content with something like the state of affairs in which one-third of our families possess in the shape of private means somewhere between a few pounds and a hundred pounds, and one-third of our families possess nothing at all or less than nothing. Our view may be that most of us are happier so, and that it is better we should live from pay-day to pay-day with virtually nothing in hand and nothing to worry about; secure and happy in the knowledge that should any trouble overtake us, all we need do is fall back upon public provisions which will be created to meet any and every personal emergency, including old age and retirement from gainful work.

My own view is that we shall have to proceed much further yet in that direction. Insecurity is the nightmare of many a low-wage working man and his wife. The cloud over all the living and doing of very many is the fear of the destitution into which they will fall should they be assailed and struck down by any one of the afflictions with which I have dealt. It has been put to me so often I feel I must believe it, that what our millions want above all else is security against destitution in the event of a mishap.

Yet I am not wholly convinced. Greater security, certainly. I have pleaded for it in previous chapters. Accident, sickness, and unemployment are public concerns and ought never to be tolerated as private visitations. But I beg leave to doubt whether peace of mind and social health can ever come from mere security against destitution. We should strive, also, if we are to have personal happiness and social health, for a state of affairs in which the typical family has sums of its own with which to further its own fancies and fortune, and from which to learn something of the technique of firmly holding and wisely using personal property.

I do not suggest, however, that every family should have its own little parcel of stocks and shares, and that every head of a family should eagerly scan the City pages every morning to see whether Kaffirs are up or Home Rails down. The management of investments is clearly too skilled a business for the average man in the street. His little nest-egg, if he is to have one, must obviously be in the Post Office Savings Bank or one of the numerous other institutions that cater for small savers.

If it is agreed that however much the State may provide social services, and however much the proportion of the national wealth falls into public hands, the average British family still needs at least some capital in the bank to tide over emergencies and misfortunes, we still have to consider how this desirable end may be achieved. The first means that springs to the mind is the time-honoured one of saving. How, then, can we augment the saving capacity of the average family, leaving aside for the moment what may happen if the monetary authorities are asinine enough not to play the right game, and bearing in mind that you can only lead a horse to the water? Some people would not save if they had an income of £1,000,000 a year.

The most obvious way of increasing saving is for everybody to spend less, or for the State to do it for them by inflating or raising the general level of prices. This, however, would involve a lowering of the general standard of living, which would be a highly retrograde step. It would be far better to raise the general level of wages if some means could be found of doing this without throwing the whole economic mechanism out of gear. As for a first instalment, it would be well worth considering the introduction of a system of family allowances, which would relieve the strain at one of the key points, the period when the family is growing up.

Another measure that might usefully be considered as a means of increasing the saving capacity of the mass of the people is the reduction of indirect taxation, especially the taxes on food, clothing, tobacco, and beer that fall so heavily on working-class families.

Then there is advertising. If we want more saving on the part of the propertyless so that we may have a more widespread ownership of wealth, we must set ourselves out to *sell* saving with all the cunning, all the zeal, all the craft, all the art, employed by the sellers of commercial goods and services.

You must enlist the services of modern publicity agents. Your advertisements must be written by people who know their job. You must canvass. You must be at least as assiduous as the demonstration salesman, the hire purchase canvasser, and the tallyman. It isn't so much the terms you offer. It is the how and when of your offer. Be on the spot when the money comes in. Get your savings share of it before there is a chance to splash it in other directions.

Or we must work through the employers; getting more and more of them to start voluntary savings schemes. Sixpence in the pound, shall we say, from the wages; into a Christmas fund, a holiday fund, an outing fund; call it what you like.

And more propaganda in the schools. Cards and the money-boxes for the children. Tell them the advantages of saving. Train them in the habit of saving. And strive to foster more mutuality clubs everywhere.

All this is already being done by the National Savings Committee with its fine apparatus of Regional Committees and their splendid companies of voluntary workers who all up and down the land inculcate and spread the saving habit. I have not the least doubt that very much of the saving that does go on among the less wealthy of our families is due directly to the efforts of these excellent and devoted people. More power to the elbows of all those engaged in this excellent work. More power and ampler means!

It is, however, little use taking trouble to ensure that the citizenry has wealth in store if we are going to look the other way while rascals freely rob and rogues freely plunder. How do we stand in this matter of safeguarding the humbler members of the community from the catch-penny tricksters who practise their frauds on him? Security against knaves and thieves is one of the first of the boons one has a right to expect from an organized society. Every citizen rightly expects justice and protection.

It has fallen to me in recent years to receive many letters from persons needing counsel or guidance in some difficulty or worry. Thousands and tens of thousands of such letters have come my way. Among them have been a constant flow of anguished appeals from persons robbed of their savings or held to some dastardly bond by knaves who live by knavery under the very shadow of our institutions for the maintenance of security and law and order.

Do you know anything of the thousands of poor women who are defrauded as a result of answering advertisements for "spare-time earning at home"?

Do you know of the fifteen shillings they borrow or scrape together and send up for "material, tools and instructions"? Do you know how the material is two yards of fourpenny muslin, the tools a penny ruler and the instructions a bit of paper telling you to cut the muslin into handkerchiefs and hem them carefully, whereupon the firm will buy them from you at a good price? Do you know how such women are being robbed and fooled day by day by tricksters about whose rascality everything is known to those who follow these doings?

Do you know of the rubbishy catch-penny correspondence courses which by high-sounding advertisements and by alluring booklets get persons who have no wish other than to improve themselves by hard work and study to sign on the dotted line, and then give them a mere pretence of tuition? The only side of these self-styled Schools and Colleges and Institutes that functions with terrible efficiency is the money-collecting side. Very seldom do they need to take a victim into court. They know just how to frighten the money out of him. Have you ever seen a full set of their circular letters sent in a timed routine to the wretch who has been caught and sold? They are known in these circles as "frighteners."

I have heard from labouring men who have signed an agreement to pay fifteen guineas at seven and six a week for instruction which would lead, they had been given to hope, to a betterment of their lot. The teaching was incomprehensible from

the first lesson; but the last penny of the last instalment has had to be paid—under threats brutal and
callous enough to send an ordinary blackmailer to
penal servitude for ten years. But it all goes on,
and on.

There are Postal Tuition Schools that are well and
honestly conducted and that give excellent value
for money. There are others which are fair to mid-
dling. And there are these of which I speak. Ought
they not all to be under the permanent surveillance
of a public department? Is there no way under
heaven by which those who turn the very wish for
personal improvement to mockery and bitter loss
can be stayed in their courses and brought to judgment?

I am doing no more than touching a scandal here
and there. But let me tell you of the advertisement
cabinets outside the little shops, small tin and glass
contraptions into which anybody who wants to
advertise "For sale a piano" or "Wanted a cook"
can put a slip of paper on payment of a few pence
a week. The cabinet is worth about seven and
sixpence. Do you know the story of most of those
cabinets you see?

You are a little shopkeeper. One day a car draws
up and two men come in to tell you a long story
about a cabinet they'd like to put up on your wall
outside. It will mean two shillings a week, you learn.
Two shillings a week. They harp on that two
shillings. Business is none too good, so you say
you're quite agreeable. They nail it up. You sign a

document. You ought to read it, but it's a very long document and they tell you it's the usual thing. Just as you sign a third man joins them so that there are three witnesses to your signature. They go away.

Thenceforward you keep in hand any sixpences you may have received from advertisers in the cabinet. You understood that you were to turn these over and you want to keep your bargain. Then one day you get a letter and a demand note. Then you discover that what you signed was an undertaking to pay *them* two shillings a week for three years.

Fifteen pounds twelve for that seven and sixpenny cabinet. You say you won't pay it. But you will. They have the law behind them. You won't pay! They'll teach you whether you'll pay or not. Into the County Court with you. Judgment for the claimants. You didn't know what you were signing! More fool you, says the Registrar. They told you wrong! That's your look-out, says the Judge. The law cannot go behind a signature, you must pay; or in due course go to gaol.

You think maybe, I'm making a song about a hole-and-corner affair? Very well. You shall hear. One of the pretty firms engaged in that business brought before one County Court in London in the course of one year over three thousand actions to force payment from wretched little shopkeepers in respect of advertisement cabinets and similar gadgets, and in over nine out of ten of the cases the decision of the Court was that the shopkeeper must pay to the last penny.

The gentlemen who employ the crooks who in the guise of travellers plant those contraptions on shopkeepers and obtaining those signatures by fraudulent misrepresentation, are able to use, for the enforcing of their pound of flesh from each, the machinery and the personnel of British Justice free, gratis, and for nothing.

I ask whether it is right and proper that the protection of poor persons against dealings of that nature should be left to the hazards of Don Quixotes of the Microphone and White Knights of the Weekly Press. Could we not have something in the nature of a Public Department to watch such doings as these? Could we not have an official who might perhaps be called the Public Prosecutor to take action where action seemed called for? Or if we cannot have a Public Prosecutor who will prosecute, could we possibly have a Public Defender who would defend? For there is no provision in our system of law and justice whereby legal assistance can be given to one infamously summoned before the County Court.

It is no use talking about the wider dissemination of wealth ownership unless you accompany whatever other action you may take with action designed to protect the humble citizen from the wiles of the knaves and rascals who now prey upon him or her without let or hindrance and with almost complete impunity.

Next on our list of expedients for increasing the capacity of the people to save must come the stopping of waste in the existing provisions for saving.

I have already spoken of the pitiful attempts of even the poorest to save something week by week. There were three purposes, you will recall, for which they felt they *must* set aside a few coins week by week. One was for hospital treatment in case of sickness or accident. No more as to that. It is covered by what I have said earlier. Then there was saving for the purchase of clothes—in some form of club. I told how we needed to extend and improve our facilities for "specific" saving of that kind—even among the very poor. The third was saving in the form of weekly payments to insurance collectors so that in the event of a death the family should be able to go into mourning and should be saved the ultimate horror of a pauper funeral.

A shilling was the most usual sum set aside by my three hundred poor families for weekly payments on burial insurance policies. A shilling. Twelve coppers, every one of them sorely needed for something else. A shilling. That in a year would have made two pounds twelve to hold or to spend.

And sixpence of that shilling went straight down the drain—wasted in collection costs, office expenses, and in the lapsing of policies. I say sixpence went down the drain; but I suspect it was far more nearly eightpence. A leaky pail indeed. More leaky than the football-pool pail; and that is leaky enough, heaven knows. Not worth sixpence, hardly worth

fourpence, in real return—the shilling collected
from the poorest of the poor. There is no cheating:
I am not saying that. There is no scandal: I am not
saying that. But waste inexcusable. A loss of
£30,000,000 a year on the £60,000,000 collected
on such policies. And all to insure the decent burial
of the family's dead.

Why cannot it go on the Health Card? A very
few pence a week would cover it all. Ten per cent
of the premiums would more than cover the working
expenses. There would be few or no lapsed policies.
And there would be a chance to introduce some sort
of order into the lamentable chaos of the burial
business.

Why not? Because never in thirty years—from
1909 to 1939—have we had a Government that dare
say a word to bring the flush of annoyance to the
cheek of the Industrial Assurance Companies. Not
the beginnings of one. The Industrial Assurance
Companies control funds to the tune of nearly
£400,000,000. Control, I say. Own, rather. It is
asking a good deal of a Government, isn't it, that it
shall speak saucily to £400,000,000? Mr. Lloyd
George is a courageous man—or was once. But
when the Insurance Companies in 1909 told him
what he might not do, he—even he—had to listen
to his master's voice.

Health Insurance was parcelled out among what
came to be called the Approved Societies, instead
of being made a national scheme parallel with
Unemployment Insurance. Funeral Benefit was

excluded from the Health Card. It is still excluded.

Perhaps it is hopeless. Perhaps we can only trust to the magnanimity of the insurance omnipotents, and hope they will be astounded at their own humanity. If so, might they not let us start by changing the "card" method of collecting insurance contributions. For every man, whether his rate is 30s. or £10 a week, whether he has worked only half a day or a full week, we make the employer stick health stamps on cards half the cost of which he deducts from the wages of the man. The man drawing £10 and the man drawing 5s. pay equal amounts. In one case it is a trifling fraction of the earnings. In the other it is a monstrous slice out of a small sum.

"But that is quite in order," say some, "the benefits are the same so the contributions should be the same." It is true that the benefits are the same; but the likelihood of drawing the benefits varies enormously. The truth of the matter is that these "social insurance" schemes of ours are not "insurance" at all. They are a special flat-rate taxation levied on a class. What I am now suggesting is that the time has come to make that a graded taxation proportionate to earnings; to make the contributions in the form of a percentage deduction from wages. Let the £10 man pay his 5s. to the fund and the £1 man pay his sixpence. Let the employer also contribute *pro rata*. Then the special taxation for social services links up with income-tax instead of being, as at present, an oddity built up piecemeal on

a rickety basis squaring with nothing else in our
theory or practice of taxation.

If we could and would do that, then we should
be well set for the next step which I now propose
with some timidity to advocate.

But go back a little. Fifty million pounds a season
have been spent on the Pools. You will not suppress
the Pools. They have flourished and they will
flourish, partly because Parliament waved its wand
the wrong way, but also because they are supplying
a need. They are satisfying a craving; the craving
for the redistribution of wealth by irrational windfalls. I ventured the opinion that Parliament would
never suppress them. I hinted that the only thing
now open was to out-pool the Pools.

Dare we consider the possibility of everyone
paying so much a week, proportionate to income,
into a pool? If the craving for redistribution of
wealth by windfalls is as deep as I take it to be, and
the willingness to forgo a part of income so that
someone, anyone, may have a windfall is as great
as I take it to be, then dare we not consider a proposal
to cater for it?

A shilling in the pound, shall we say, of all income
into a pool, out of which lovely damsels in smart
uniforms shall draw blindfold, once a week or once
a month, so many names of so many Toms, Dicks,
and Harrys, so many Peggies, Joans, and Kates,
each one of whom shall thereupon get—what
shall we say?—a thousand pounds.

There is an idea that everyone who has won a

large prize in the Pools has played the fool with it. The assurance with which this is stated is usually a measure of the ignorance. Some play the fool. Some play the goat. But a good many, I am told, show admirable control and discernment.

Does anyone know what has, in fact, happened to say a random sample of a thousand big-prize winners in the Pools? No one! What momentous matters there are upon which our systematized knowledge amounts to next to nothing!

But the effect on morale! Well, it may be that the wish and the hope for a windfall right out of the blue might make even more of us than now go about life gaping at the sky till we get a crick in the neck instead of minding where we're going. It might. On the other hand it might not. It might answer some need within us and make us settle down to good management while we hold ourselves ready for the good luck.

And now, with the sound of windfalls in our ears —having only a moment ago chased the insurance companies off the public stage so far as their paltry burial business is concerned—let us welcome them back to play a nobler and a better part. Let them have done with these burial pennies! Leave that to the State! And get on with endowment business instead.

There is no need to dismiss any collectors. No need to contract any staffs. Let the companies collect for endowment. If they want State aid, State backing, State subsidies even, to make the transition

easy and to make the endowments advantageous
and alluring, I for one shall be in favour of giving
them anything in reason they may ask for—provided
of course public aid is conditioned by public control.
And if they will introduce into every endowment
scheme the principle of the periodic drawing of lots
in accordance with which some endowments shall
be paid at once instead of years ahead, then I
become not merely an advocate but an enthusiast.

At present we have nothing, nothing whatsoever,
in the whole range of our social services machinery
which provides for the payment of a nice lump sum.
I would like to see that taboo broken. I would like
to see it tried. I have talked about the thriftless and
the shiftless, and the feckless. But they never had a
lump sum. Suppose you try them!

But why at random, I may be asked. Why not
lump sums at predetermined dates? This is why.
Because we are most of us so made that if we know
when the lump sum is coming we borrow on our
expectations and when it comes it merely goes to
pay our debts.

Employers in Indian factories, in a desperate
attempt to smash the debt system, tried keeping
back a percentage on wages and paid it over in a
lump sum. But it was all pledged. Do not forget the
woman who sprang up with a novel business at
Woolwich. She bought, from Co-op members, their
divi checks which were to mature at quarter-end.
She gave the member a portion of the value as ready
money. And she herself later cashed the divi cheque

and enriched herself with the balance. If you know when the lump sum is coming, and you are sure of it, you will find you have been offered means of raising the wind on it long before it comes. But if you don't know, you can't.

If you say you will have nothing to do with anything so immoral as drawing and distributing by lot, remember, I beg of you, that some millions of our families have no margin at all to save on. What about them? Will you leave them to relief, supplemented by the wild chance of a win in the Pools? You see, I was providing for something apart from individual saving—which for these could mean nothing or next to nothing. I was giving them at least *a chance* in a supplementary system of automatic redistribution. You are still offering them nothing but relief from destitution.

We have now considered several ways of making capital more widely available by increasing the power of the average citizen to save. He may not, of course, take these opportunities. He may be a born spendthrift, but at least these measures, if adopted, would enable those who wanted to save to save.

There is, however, another way of redistributing the capital resources of the nation, to take from those who have too much and give to those who have too little.

In one way as I have said, this is going on all the time. The Chancellor of the Exchequer taxes the rich through income-tax, surtax, and death duties and redistributes the money impartially in the form of social services or spends it on such objects of communal concern as national defence. This is a thoroughly praiseworthy development, and should be encouraged.

There is, however, another way, a way that has a fair number of adherents, but a way that seems to me to be outside practical politics, and that is confiscation. It would be possible forcibly to redistribute the privately owned wealth of this country so that everybody had his £1,500. It would not last for long, of course. Your clever money-maker would soon contrive to fructify his share and your born spendthrift would even sooner contrive to lose his.

It will, however, be objected by those who propose such wholesale confiscation that they never thought of so fantastic an idea as redistributing the national wealth in this way to individuals. What they have in mind is something quite different, the nationalization of the means of production. Here again we come up against a brick wall. Any proposal to take the wealth from its present owners by force and parcel it out would mean, to speak euphemistically, a lot of unpleasantness. Then you might really see somebody hanging from a lamp-post in Whitehall. I see no prospect of the people of Britain backing such action or of allowing any jack-booted gang of shirted mugs to do it in the people's name against the people's will.

In my last pages I should like to try to restate

something that has been at the back of my mind
all the time, and which has underlain all that I have
written in this book, and that is that the present
disparity in the ownership of wealth in this country
is due in no small degree to the ridiculous plutolatry,
or worship of wealth, to which we as a nation are
so prone. Rich men are looked up to by far too many
people because they are rich, and irrespective of any
personal worth they may have. This is not a healthy
sign. It is not found in the new countries, our
Dominions overseas. There a man is respected if
and because he can do something, not because his
grandfather speculated successfully on the Stock
Exchange, or because a more remote ancestor
reaved somebody else's cattle or snaffled monastic
lands four hundred years ago.

I think something of this spirit is spreading
more widely abroad in this country. People are
getting, I fancy, just a little more suspicious of
how other people acquired their wealth. There is
more regard for a man like Lord Nuffield, who has
made every penny of his millions by sheer ability,
than for any one of those numerous dukes whose
rent rolls are so big because of their forbears' acquisi-
tive skill. There will, I hope, come to be different
standards for judging the acquisition of wealth and
the use of it. In every age great fortunes will be piled
up. George Baylis made a cool quarter of a million
out of farming in the blackest days of the depression
of the last century. There will always be such men.
Provided their methods are fair there can be no

cavil against such money-makers. They are invariably able men and should be respected. In many cases Lord Nuffield is an outstanding example among those still living, and Sir Halley Stewart, the founder of these lectures, is another; they prove to be great public benefactors.

The use of wealth, however, should be judged quite differently from its making. An earned fortune is its owner's reward for outstanding ability, or just occasionally for outstanding luck, but an unearned fortune should be regarded as a public trust. Society entrusts certain property to a man because his ancestors earned it (in some cases by exceedingly questionable means) and protects him from spoliation. In return society has a right to demand that that wealth be used in a manner consonant with the social welfare. If it is land, it must be kept in good heart and adequately equipped with stock and buildings. If it is industrial capital, it must be kept in good running order. Great incomes anti-socially squandered deserve an inquest by society into their ownership.

What is the moral of all this? What conclusions can we draw from all that I have said in this book? Is the *status quo* satisfactory? I have failed abysmally if by now you still think that. What then can we do to change the *status quo*? I have outlined a good many suggestions for spreading the corpus of privately owned wealth more evenly over the populace of this country. Higher wages, family allowances, more savings propaganda, more social services, fewer wastes, fewer fraudulent practices, all have a part to play. But there is something else. Something intangible. Something that I have hinted at in these last few paragraphs.

It is a change of heart that is really needed. That is what the great founder of Christianity taught two thousand years ago. It is still true to-day. Doubly true. A change of heart that would make the owners of wealth ashamed to dally for one moment while misery and want remained, if not on their doorsteps then just around the corner.

There is too much that is selfish and meretricious in our civilization to-day. Our scale of values is warped and garish. For far too many people the world is not worth having a stake in. They feel the dice are loaded against them. Only the Pools seem to be impartial. You always know of somebody whose pal's girl's pal's boy has won something. You never seem to hear of anybody who has much of a break any other way. All above you is a closed ring, a selfish monopoly of wealth. Is it a wonder that our ideals have gone all awry?

Then there is the inevitable international situation. Any day we may all be blown to glory. Why bother to be moral? Why bother to do anything lasting and worth while? Was there ever greater inducement to eat, drink, and be merry?

In all this welter of frustration and tinsel ideology the still small voice can be heard, suggesting that if we want people to have a stake in the world, if we want them to have the will to save and strive and do worthwhile things, then we must make them a world worth having a stake in, a world worth saving and striving in, and where the doing of worthwhile things will reap its merited reward. As Burke said a century and a half ago, if you want to make people love their country you must make the country a country worth loving.

This is not a counsel of perfection. We are all of us responsible for the world as it is to-day. We cannot shake off that responsibility. We all contribute our jot to the state of domestic frustration and international tension that blights the world to-day. It is up to all of us to exert ourselves more than we have done hitherto to clear up the mess. We may not be able to move mountains, or dictators, at once. But we can start that process of changing of heart without which no effort is going to succeed. We can each of us help to prepare the seed-bed in which a happier order of things can germinate. That is a privilege of every individual that a thousand knouts and a sea of castor oil cannot eradicate.

The end of this book may appear to have got rather far from its beginning, but it is not really so. The maldistribution of the privately ownable wealth of this country is but a symptom of a universal malaise. We are, perhaps, as H. G. Wells has suggested, at the turning-point in the history of man as a species. Let us take thought before it is too late.

THE END